D1228397

AN INTRODUCTION TO LOAD BEARING BRICKWORK DESIGN

ELLIS HORWOOD SERIES IN ENGINEERING SCIENCE

STRENGTH OF MATERIALS
J. M. ALEXANDER, University College of Swansea.
TECHNOLOGY OF ENGINEERING MANUFACTURE
J. M. ALEXANDER, R. C. BREWER, Imperial College of Science and Technology, University of London, J. R. CROOKALL, Cranfield Institute of Technology.
VIBRATION ANALYSIS AND CONTROL SYSTEM DYNAMICS
CHRISTOPHER BEARDS, Imperial College of Science and Technology, University of London.
COMPUTER AIDED DESIGN AND MANUFACTURE
C. B. BESANT, Imperial College of Science and Technology, University of London.
STRUCTURAL DESIGN AND SAFETY
D. I. BLOCKLEY, University of Bristol.
BASIC LUBRICATION THEORY 3rd Edition
ALASTAIR CAMERON, Imperial College of Science and Technology, University of London.
STRUCTURAL MODELLING AND OPTIMIZATION
D. G. CARMICHAEL, University of Western Australia
ADVANCED MECHANICS OF MATERIALS 2nd Edition
Sir HUGH FORD, F.R.S., Imperial College of Science and Technology, University of London and J. M. ALEXANDER, University College of Swansea.
ELASTICITY AND PLASTICITY IN ENGINEERING
Sir HUGH FORD, F.R.S. and R. T. FENNER, Imperial College of Science and Technology, University of London.
INTRODUCTION TO LOADBEARING BRICKWORK
A. W. HENDRY, B. A. SINHA and S. R. DAVIES, University of Edinburgh
ANALYSIS AND DESIGN OF CONNECTIONS BETWEEN STRUCTURAL JOINTS
M. HOLMES and L. H. MARTIN, University of Aston in Birmingham
TECHNIQUES OF FINITE ELEMENTS
BRUCE M. IRONS, University of Calgary, and S. AHMAD, Bangladesh University of Engineering and Technology, Dacca.
FINITE ELEMENT PRIMER
BRUCE IRONS and N. SHRIVE, University of Calgary
PROBABILITY FOR ENGINEERING DECISIONS: A Bayesian Approach
I. J. JORDAAN, University of Calgary
STRUCTURAL DESIGN OF CABLE-SUSPENDED ROOFS
L. KOLLAR, City Planning Office, Budapest and K. SZABO, Budapest Technical University.
CONTROL OF FLUID POWER, 2nd Edition
D. McCLOY, The Northern Ireland Polytechnic and H. R. MARTIN, University of Waterloo, Ontario, Canada.
TUNNELS: Planning, Design, Construction
T. M. MEGAW and JOHN BARTLETT, Mott, Hay and Anderson, International Consulting Engineers
UNSTEADY FLUID FLOW
R. PARKER, University College, Swansea
DYNAMICS OF MECHANICAL SYSTEMS 2nd Edition
J. M. PRENTIS, University of Cambridge.
ENERGY METHODS IN VIBRATION ANALYSIS
T. H. RICHARDS, University of Aston, Birmingham.
ENERGY METHODS IN STRESS ANALYSIS: With an Introduction to Finite Element Techniques
T. H. RICHARDS, University of Aston, Birmingham.
ROBOTICS AND TELECHIRICS
M. W. THRING, Queen Mary College, University of London
STRESS ANALYSIS OF POLYMERS 2nd Edition
J. G. WILLIAMS, Imperial College of Science and Technology, University of London.

AN INTRODUCTION TO LOAD BEARING BRICKWORK DESIGN

A. W. HENDRY, B.Sc., Ph.D., D.Sc., F.I.C.E. F.I.Struct.E., F.R.S.E.
B. P. SINHA, B.Sc., Ph.D., M.I.Struct.E., M.I.C.E., C.Eng.
and
S. R. DAVIES, B.Sc., Ph.D., M.I.C.E., C.Eng.
Department of Civil Engineering and Building Science
University of Edinburgh

ELLIS HORWOOD LIMITED
Publishers · Chichester

Halsted Press: a division of
JOHN WILEY & SONS
New York · Chichester · Brisbane · Toronto

First published in 1981 by

ELLIS HORWOOD LIMITED

Market Cross House, Cooper Street, Chichester, West Sussex, PO19 1EB, England

The publisher's colophon is reproduced from James Gillison's drawing of the ancient Market Cross, Chichester.

Distributors:

Australia, New Zealand, South-east Asia:
Jacaranda-Wiley Ltd., Jacaranda Press,
JOHN WILEY & SONS INC.,
G.P.O. Box 859, Brisbane, Queensland 40001, Australia

Canada:
JOHN WILEY & SONS CANADA LIMITED
22 Worcester Road, Rexdale, Ontario, Canada.

Europe, Africa:
JOHN WILEY & SONS LIMITED
Baffins Lane, Chichester, West Sussex, England.

North and South America and the rest of the world:
Halsted Press: a division of
JOHN WILEY & SONS
605 Third Avenue, New York, N.Y. 10016, U.S.A.

© **1981 A. W. Hendry, B. P. Sinha and S. R. Davies/Ellis Horwood Ltd.**

British Library Cataloguing in Publication Data
Hendry, A. W.
    An introduction to load bearing brickwork design. —
    (Ellis Horwood series in mechanical and civil engineering)
    1. Building, Brick
    2. Structural dynamics
    I. Title   II. Sinha, B. P.
    III. Davies, S. R.
    624.1'836   TA679

Library of Congress Card No.   81–4121   AACR2

ISBN 0-85312-216-4 (Ellis Horwood Ltd., Publishers — Library Edn.)
ISBN 0-85312-355-1 (Ellis Horwood Ltd., Publishers — Student Edn.)
ISBN 0-470-27227-9 (Halsted Press)

Typeset in Press Roman by Ellis Horwood Ltd.
Printed in Great Britain by R. J. Acford, Chichester.

Table of Contents

Author's Preface 11

Chapter 1 – Loadbearing Brickwork Buildings
1.1   Advantages and development of loadbearing brickwork 13
1.2   Basic design considerations 13
1.3   Structural safety: Limit state design 17
1.4   Foundations 19

Chapter 2 – Bricks and Mortars
2.1   Introduction 20
2.2   Bricks 20
      2.2.1   Compressive strength 25
      2.2.2   Absorption 25
      2.2.3   Frost resistance 25
      2.2.4   Dimensional changes 27
              2.2.4.1   Thermal movement 27
              2.2.4.2   Moisture movement 27
      2.2.5   Soluble salts 28
              2.2.5.1   Efflorescence 28
              2.2.5.2   Sulphate attack 29
      2.2.6   Fire resistance 29
2.3   Mortar 29
      2.3.1   Function and requirement of mortar 29
      2.3.2   Cement 29
2.4   Lime: Non-hydraulic or Semi-hydraulic Lime 31
2.5   Sand 33
2.6   Water 33
2.7   Plasticised Portland cement mortar 33
2.8   Use of pigments 33
2.9   Frost inhibitors 33
2.10 Proportioning and strength 34
2.11 Choice of unit and mortar 35
2.12 Wall ties 35

Chapter 3 — Brick Masonry Properties
3.1   General 39
3.2   Compressive strength 39
   3.2.1   Indications from standard tests 39
   3.2.2   The interaction of brick and bed material. 41
   3.2.3   Formulae for brickwork strength based on elastic analysis. 42
   3.2.4   Failure criterion based on biaxial strength of bricks and mortar .45
   3.2.5   Experimental measurement of brick masonry
           compressive strength 46
3.3   Strength of brickwork in combined shear and compression 47
3.4   Strength of brickwork subject to biaxial stress 48
   3.4.1   Brickwork subject to biaxial stresses 48
   3.4.2   Failure criteria under complex stresses. 50
3.5   The tensile strength of brickwork 50
   3.5.1   Direct tensile strength 50
   3.5.2   Flexural tensile strength 51
3.6   Stress-strain properties of brickwork 52
3.7   Effects of workmanship on brickwork strength 53

Chapter 4 — A Code of Practice for Loadbearing Brickwork: BS 5628
4.1   Codes of practice: general 55
4.2   The basis and structure of BS 5628. 55
   4.2.1   Section 1: General. 56
   4.2.2   Section 2: Materials, components, symbols, etc. 56
   4.2.3   Sections 3 and 4: Design. 57
   4.2.4   Section 5: Accidental damage 68

Chapter 5 — Design for Compressive Loading
5.1   Introduction. 69
5.2   Wall and column behaviour under axial load 69
5.3   Wall and column behaviour under eccentric load 70
5.4   Slenderness ratio 71
   5.4.1   Effective height. 71
   5.4.2   Effective thickness. 73
5.5   Calculation of eccentricity 75
   5.5.1   Approximate method. 75
   5.5.2   Frame analysis 77
5.6   Vertical load resistance. 78
   5.6.1   Design vertical load resistance of walls. 78
   5.6.2   Design vertical load resistance of columns 78
   5.6.3   Design vertical load resistance of cavity walls or columns 81
   5.6.4   Design vertical strength for concentrated loads 82

5.7 Vertical loading. 83
5.8 Modification factors. 83
   5.8.1 Small plan area 83
   5.8.2 Narrow brick walls. 83
5.9 Examples. 84

Chapter 6 – Design for Wind Loading
6.1 Introduction. 90
6.2 Overall stability. 90
6.3 Theoretical methods for wind load analysis 91
   6.3.1 Coupled shear walls 93
   6.3.2 Cantilever approach 93
   6.3.3 Equivalent frame. 93
   6.3.4 Wide column frame 95
   6.3.5 Continuum. 95
   6.3.6 Finite element analysis 95
   6.3.7 Selection of analytical method. 95
6.4 Load distribution between unsymmetrically arranged shear walls . . .99

Chapter 7 – Lateral Load Analysis of Brickwork Panels
7.1 General 103
7.2 Analysis of panels with precompression 103
   7.2.1 Flexural tensile strength 103
   7.2.2 Initial precompression 103
   7.2.3 Stiffness of a building. 104
   7.2.4 Boundary conditions 106
7.3 An approximate theory for the lateral load analysis of walls 107
   7.3.1 Wall with returns. 108
7.4 Effect of very high precompression. 113
7.5 Lateral load design of panels without precompression. 113
   7.5.1 Vertically or horizontally spanning panels 113
   7.5.2 Panels supported on more than two sides with various boun-
       dary conditions. 114
   7.5.3 Fracture line analysis 115
   7.5.4 BS 5628 bending moment coefficients for fracture line
       analysis 117

Chapter 8 – Composite Action between Walls and other Elements
8.1 Composite wall beams 120
   8.1.1 Introduction. 120

8.1.2   Development of design methods. 121
8.1.3   Basic assumptions 123
8.1.4   The Graphical method 124
    8.1.4.1   Maximum vertical stress in wall 124
    8.1.4.2   Axial force in the beam 125
    8.1.4.3   Maximum shear stress along interface 126
    8.1.4.4   Bending moments in the beam 126
8.2   Interaction between wall panels and frames 131
  8.2.1   Introduction. 131
  8.2.2   Design method based on plastic failure modes. 133
    8.2.2.1   Introduction. 133
    8.2.2.2   Design procedure. 133
    8.2.2.3   Example 135
    8.2.2.4   Additional considerations 136

Chapter 9 – Design for Accidental Damage

9.1   Introduction. 137
9.2   Accidental loading. 137
9.3   Likelihood of occurrence of progressive collapse 139
9.4   Possible methods of design 141
9.5   Use of ties 142
  9.5.1   Vertical ties 142
  9.5.2   Horizontal ties 143
    9.5.2.1   Peripheral ties. 143
    9.5.2.2   Internal ties 143
    9.5.2.3   External wall or column ties 144
    9.5.2.4   Examples. 145

**Chapter 10 – Design Calculations for a Seven-Storey Dormitory Building
                according to BS 5628**

10.1 Introduction. 147
10.2 Basis of design 149
  10.2.1 Loadings 149
10.3 Quality control. 149
  10.3.1 Partial safety factors for materials. 149
10.4 Calculation of vertical loading on walls 150
10.5 Wind loading 152
  10.5.1 General stability 152
  10.5.2 Wind loads. 152
  10.5.3 Assumed section of wall resisting the wind moment 154
10.6 Design loads. 158
  10.6.1 Load combinations: Wall A 158

10.6.1.1 Selection of brick and mortar combinations for Wall A. . 164
10.6.2 Load combinations: Wall B 165
10.6.2.1 Selection of brick and mortar for innerleaf of Wall B . . . 166
10.6.2.2 Calculation of eccentricity 166
10.6.2.3 Design of outer leaf of Wall B 169
10.7 Design of panel for lateral loading. 173
10.7.1 Limiting dimension 173
10.7.2 Characteristic wind load 174
10.8 Design for accidental damage. 175
10.8.1 Introduction. 175
10.8.2 Protected wall. 175
10.8.3 Accidental damage: options. 176
10.8.4 Design calculations for option 2 176
10.8.5 Vertical elements. 178

Definition of Terms used in Brickwork 179

Further Reading and Reference 182

Index 183

Authors' Preface

The structural use of brick masonry has to some extent been hampered by its long history as a craft based material and some years ago its disappearance as a structural material was being predicted. The fact that this has not happened is a result of the inherent advantages of brickwork and the design of brick masonry structures has shown steady development, based on the results of continuing research in many countries. Nevertheless, structural brickwork is not used as widely as it could be and one reason for this lies in the fact that design in this medium is not taught in many engineering schools alongside steel and concrete. To help to improve this situation, the authors have written this book especially for students in university and polytechnic courses in structural engineering and for young graduates preparing for professional examination in structural design.

The text attempts to explain the basic principles of brickwork design, the essential properties of the materials used, the design of various structural elements and the procedure in carrying out the design of a complete building. In practice, the basic data and methodology for structural design in a given material is contained in a code of practice and in illustrating design procedures it is necessary to relate these to a particular document of this kind. In the present case the standard referred to, and discussed in some detail, is the British BS 5628 Part 1, which was first published in 1978. This code is based on limit state principles which have been familiar to many designers through their application to reinforced concrete design but which are summarised in the text.

No attempt has been made in this introductory book to give extensive lists of references but a short list of material for further study is included which will permit the reader to follow up any particular topic in greater depth.

Preparation of this book has been based on a study of the work of a large number of research workers and practising engineers to whom the authors acknowledge their indebtedness. In particular, they wish to express their thanks to the following for permission to reproduce material from their publications, as identified in the text; British Standards Institution; Institution of Civil Engineers; The Building Research Establishment; Structural Clay Products Ltd.

A. W. Hendry
B. P. Sinha
S. R. Davies
Edinburgh June 1981

CHAPTER 1

Loadbearing Brickwork Buildings

1.1 ADVANTAGES AND DEVELOPMENT OF LOADBEARING BRICKWORK

The basic advantage of brickwork construction is that it is possible to use the same element to perform a variety of functions which in a steel frame building, for example, have to be provided for separately, with consequent complication in detailed construction. Thus brickwork may, simultaneously, provide structure, subdivision of space, thermal and acoustic insulation as well as fire and weather protection. As a material, it is relatively cheap but durable and produces external wall finishes of very acceptable appearance. Brickwork construction is flexible in terms of building layout and can be constructed without very large capital expenditure on the part of the builder.

In the first half of the present century brick construction for multi-storey buildings was very largely displaced by steel and reinforced concrete framed structures, although these were very often clad in brick. One of the main reasons for this was that until around 1950 loadbearing walls were proportioned by purely empirical rules which led to excessively thick walls which were wasteful of space and material and took a great deal of time to build. The situation changed in a number of countries after 1950 with the introduction of structural codes of practice which made it possible to calculate the necessary wall thickness and masonry strengths on a more rational basis. These codes of practice were based on research programmes and building experience, and although initially limited in scope provided a sufficient basis for the design of buildings of twenty stories. A considerable amount of research and practical experience over the past twenty years has led to the improvement and refinement of the various structural codes. As a result, the structural design of brick masonry buildings is approaching a level similar to that applying to steel and concrete.

1.2 BASIC DESIGN CONSIDERATIONS

Loadbearing brickwork construction is most appropriately used for buildings in which the floor area is subdivided into a relatively large number of rooms of small to medium size and in which the floor plan is repeated on each storey

throughout the height of the building. These considerations give ample oppor-
tunity for disposing loadbearing walls, continuous from foundation to roof level,
and, because of the moderate floor spans, not called upon to carry unduly heavy
concentrations of vertical load. The types of buildings which are compatible
with these requirements include flats, hostels, hotels and other residential buildings.

The form and wall-layout for a particular building will evolve from functional
requirements and site conditions and will call for collaboration between engineer
and architect. The arrangement chosen will not usually be critical from the
structural point of view provided that a reasonable balance is allowed between
walls oriented in the principal directions of the building so as to permit the
development of adequate resistance to lateral forces in both of these directions.
Very unsymmetrical arrangements should be avoided as these will give rise to
torsional effects under lateral loading which will be difficult to calculate and
which may produce undesirable stress distributions.

Stair wells, lift shafts and service ducts play an important part in deciding
layout and are often of primary importance in providing lateral rigidity.

The great variety of possible wall arrangements in a brickwork building
makes it rather difficult to define distinct types of structure, but a rough
classification might be made as follows:

    (a) Cellular wall systems
    (b) Simple or double cross-wall systems
    (c) Complex arrangements.

A cellular arrangement is one in which both internal and external walls are
loadbearing and in which these walls form a cellular pattern in plan. Fig. 1.1(a)
shows an example of such a wall layout.

The second category includes simple cross-wall structures in which the
main bearing walls are at right angles to the longitudinal axis of the building.
The floor slabs span between the main cross-walls, and longitudinal stability is
achieved by means of corridor walls, as shown in Fig. 1.1(b). This type of
structure is suitable for a hostel or hotel building having a large number of
identical rooms. The outer walls may be clad in non-loadbearing brickwork or
with other materials.

It will be observed that there is a limit to the depth of building which can
be constructed on the cross-wall principle if the rooms are to have effective
day-lighting. If a deeper block with a service core is required a somewhat more
complex system of cross-walls set parallel to both major axes of the building
may be used, as in Fig. 1.1(c).

All kinds of hybrids between cellular and cross-wall arrangements are
possible, and these are included under the heading 'complex', a typical example
being shown in Fig. 1.1(d).

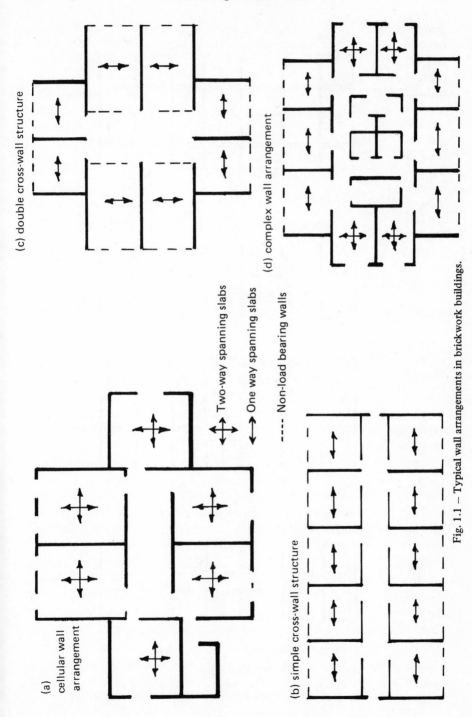

Fig. 1.1 – Typical wall arrangements in brickwork buildings.

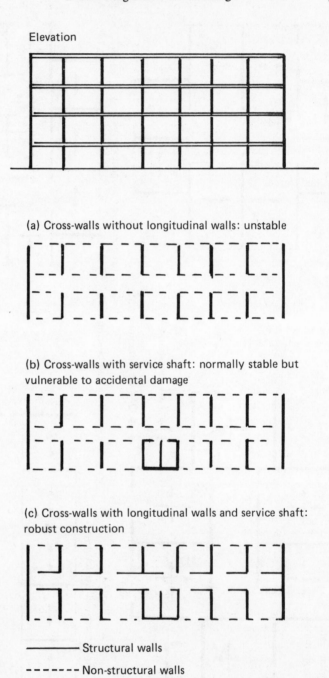

Elevation

(a) Cross-walls without longitudinal walls: unstable

(b) Cross-walls with service shaft: normally stable but vulnerable to accidental damage

(c) Cross-walls with longitudinal walls and service shaft: robust construction

———————— Structural walls

- - - - - - - Non-structural walls

Fig. 1.2 – Liability of a simple cross-wall structure to accidental damage.

Considerable attention has been devoted in recent years to the necessity for ensuring the 'robustness' of buildings. This has arisen from a number of building failures in which although the individual members have been adequate in terms of resisting their normal service loads, yet the building as a whole has suffered severe damage from abnormal loading, resulting for example from a gas explosion or from vehicle impact. It is impossible to quantify loads of this kind, and what is required is to construct buildings in such a way that an incident of this category does not result in catastrophic collapse, out of proportion to the initial forces. Meeting this requirement begins with the selection of wall layout since some arrangements are inherently more resistant to abnormal forces than others. This point is illustrated in Fig. 1.2 : a building consisting only of floor slabs and cross-walls (Fig. 1.2(a)) is obviously unstable and liable to collapse under the influence of small lateral forces acting parellel to its longer axis. This particular weakness could be removed by incorporating a lift shaft or stair well to provide resistance in the weak direction, as in Fig. 1.2(b). However, the flank or gable walls are still vulnerable, for example to vehicle impact, and limited damage to this wall on the lowermost storey would result in the collapse of a large section of the building.

A building having a wall layout as in Fig. 1.2(c) on the other hand is clearly much more resistant to all kinds of disturbing forces, having a high degree of lateral stability and unlikely to suffer extensive damage from failure of any particular wall.

Robustness is not, however, purely a matter of wall layout. Thus a floor system consisting of unconnected precast planks will be much less resistant to damage than one which has cast-in-situ concrete floors with two-way reinforcement. Similarly, the detailing of elements and their connections is of great importance. For example, adequate bearing of beams and slabs on walls is essential in a gravity structure to prevent possible failure not only from local over-stressing but also from relative movement between walls and other elements. Such movement could result from foundation settlement, thermal or moisture movements. An extreme case occurs in seismic areas where positive tying together of walls and floors is essential.

Codes of practice give some guidance on these matters but can never be a substitute for care and vigilance on the part of the designer.

1.3 STRUCTURAL SAFETY: LIMIT STATE DESIGN

The objective of ensuring a fundamentally stable or robust building, as discussed in section 1.2 is an aspect of structural safety. The measures adopted in pursuit of this objective are to a large extent qualitative and conceptual whereas the method of ensuring satisfactory structural performance in resisting service loads is dealt with in a more quantitative manner, essentially by trying to relate estimates of these loads with estimates of material strength and rigidity.

The basic aim of structural design is to ensure that a structure should fulfil its intended function throughout its lifetime without excessive deflection, cracking or collapse. The engineer is expected to meet this aim with due regard to economy and durability. It is recognised, however, that it is not possible to design structures which will meet these requirements in all conceivable circumstances, at least within the limits of financial feasibility. For example, it is not expected that normally designed structures will be capable of resisting conceivable but improbable accidents which would result in catastrophic damage, such as impact of a large aircraft. It is, on the other hand, accepted that there is uncertainty in the estimation of service loads on stuctures, that the strength of construction materials is variable, and that the means of relating loads to strength are at best approximations. It is possible that an unfavourable combination of these circumstances could result in structural failure; design procedures should, therefore, ensure that the probability of such a failure is acceptably small.

The question then arises as to what probability of failure is 'acceptably small'. Investigation of accident statistics suggests that, in the context of buildings, a one in a million chance of failure leading to a fatality will be, if not explicitly acceptable to the public, at least such as to give rise to little concern. In recent years, therefore, structural design has aimed, indirectly, to provide levels of safety consistent with a probability of failure of this order.

Consideration of levels of safety in structural design is a recent development and has been applied through the concept of 'limit state' design. The definition of a limit state is that a structure becomes unfit for its intended purpose when it reaches that particular condition. A limit state may be one of complete failure (ultimate limit state) or it may define a condition of excessive deflection or cracking (serviceability limit state). The advantage of this approach is that it permits the definition of direct criteria for strength and serviceability taking into account the uncertainties of loading, strength, and structural analysis as well as questions such as the consequences of failure.

The essential principles of limit state design may be summarised as follows: considering the ultimate limit state of a particular structure, for failure to occur:

$$R^* - S^* \leqslant 0 \qquad\qquad (1.1)$$

where $R^* = \dfrac{R_k}{\gamma_m}$ = Design strength of the structure, and

$S^* = f(\gamma_f . Q_k)$ = Design loading effects

where γ_m and γ_f are *partial safety factors*. R_k and Q_k are *characteristic values* of resistance and load actions, generally chosen such that 95% of samples representing R_k will exceed this value and 95% of the applied forces will be less than Q_k.

The probability of failure is then:

$$P[R^* - S^* \leqslant 0] = p \quad . \tag{1.3}$$

If a value of p, say 10^{-6}, is prescribed it is possible to calculate values of the partial safety factors, γ_m and γ_f, in the limit state equation which would be consistent with this probability of failure. In order to do this, however, it is necessary to define the load effects and structural resistance in statistical terms, which in practice is rarely possible. The partial safety factors, therefore, cannot be calculated in a precise way and have to be determined on the basis of construction experience, and laboratory testing against a background of statistical theory. The application of the limit state approach as exemplified by the British Code of Practice BS 5628 is discussed in Chapter 4.

1.4 FOUNDATIONS

Building structures in load-bearing brickwork are characteristically stiff in the vertical direction and have a limited tolerance for differential movement of foundations. Studies of existing buildings have suggested that the maximum relative deflection (i.e. the ratio of deflection to the length of the deflected part) in the the walls of multi-storeyed loadbearing brickwork buildings should not exceed 0.0003 in sand or hard clay and 0.0004 in soft clay. These figures apply to walls whose length exceeds three times their height. It has also been suggested that the maximum average settlement of a brickwork building should not exceed 150mm. These figures, are, however, purely indicative, and a great deal depends on the rate of settlement as well as on the characteristics of the brickwork. Settlement calculations by normal soil mechanics techniques will indicate whether these limits are likely to be exceeded. Where problems have arisen, the cause has usually been associated with particular types of clay soils which are subject to excessive shrinkage in periods of dry weather. In these soils the foundations should be at a depth of not less than 1 m in order to avoid moisture fluctuations.

High-rise brickwork buildings are usually built on a reinforced concrete raft of about 600 mm thickness. The wall system stiffens the raft and helps to ensure uniform ground pressures, whilst the limitation on floor spans which applies to brickwork structures has the effect of minimising the amount of reinforcement required in the foundation slab. Under exceptionally good soil conditions it may be possible to use spread footings, whilst very unfavourable conditions may necessitate piling with ground beams.

CHAPTER 2

Bricks and Mortars

2.1 INTRODUCTION

Brick masonry is a well proven building material possessing excellent properties in terms of appearance, durability and cost in comparison with alternatives. However, the quality of the masonry in a building depends on the materials used, and hence all brickwork materials must conform to certain minimum standards. The basic components of brickwork are brick and mortar, the latter being in itself a composite of cement, lime and sand and sometimes of other constituents. The object of this chapter is to describe the properties of the various materials making up brick masonry.

2.2 BRICKS

Fired clay bricks must conform to relevant national standards, for example in the United Kingdom to BS 3921. In this standard the following classes of bricks are defined:

i) *Common bricks,* suitable for general building work
ii) *Facing bricks,* used for exterior and interior walls and available in variety of textures and colours
iii) *Engineering bricks* are dense and strong with defined limits of absorption and compressive strength as given in Table 2.3

Bricks are also classified according to the quality and use:

i) *Internal:* These bricks are suitable for internal use. They must be free from deep and extensive cracks and also from expansive particles of lime. They are suitable for rendering but unsuitable for work where good appearance 'fair face' is required. Moderate efflorescence is permitted, but there is no special requirement for soluble salts content or frost resistance.
ii) *Ordinary:* These bricks are well fired and have similar requirements as internal, and under normal conditions of exposure are durable in the external face of a building.

iii) *Special:* These bricks are hard fired and are durable in extreme conditions of exposure to water and freezing. Special quality bricks must conform to the limit prescribed by BS 3921 for maximum soluble salt content given in Table 2.1. All engineering and some facing or common bricks may come under this category.

Table 2.1 Maximum salt content of 'special quality' brick (BS 3921)

Soluble radicals	Maximum content percentage by weight as tested on ten brick samples
Sulphate	0.50
Calcium	0.30
Magnesium	0.03
Potassium	0.03
Sodium	0.03

Bricks may be wire cut, with or without perforations, or pressed with single or double frogs. The bricks having frogs not exceeding 20% of the total volume or perforation not exceeding 25% are classified as 'solid'. Perforated bricks contain holes less than 20 mm wide or less than 500 mm^2 in cross-section and the volume of perforations exceeds 25% of the total volume of bricks. In the United Kingdom 180 mm 'Calculon', calcium silicate or concrete bricks are also used, covered by BS 187 and BS 1180. 'Calculon' bricks are manufactured in three strength grades as given in Table 2.2.

Table 2.2 Grade and Compressive strength of Calculon Bricks

Grade	Average compressive strength N/mm^2	Average wt. in kg.	Perforations in %
A10	68.9 ⎫	4.09	23
B75	51.7 ⎬		
C5	34.5	3.95	Solid

Bricks of shapes other than rectangular prisms are referred to as 'standard special' and are covered by BS 4729. These bricks should not be confused with 'special' bricks mentioned earlier in this section.

Different varieties of bricks are shown in Figs. 2.1 and 2.2.

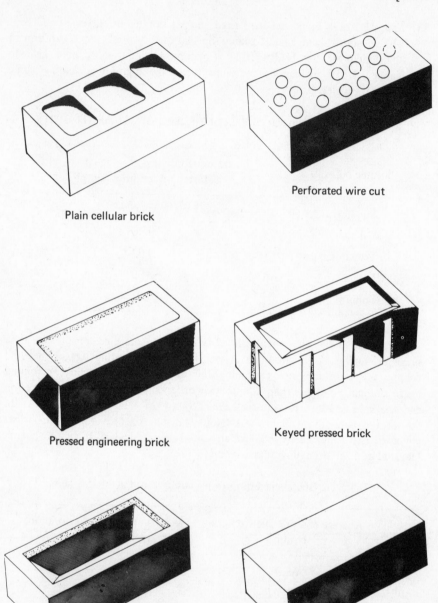

Plain cellular brick

Perforated wire cut

Pressed engineering brick

Keyed pressed brick

Pressed brick with frog

Solid wire cut

Fig. 2.1 – Types of standard bricks.

Calculon 5

Calculon 10

Calculon 75

Fig. 2.2 – Calculon Bricks.

Table 2.3 *Classification of bricks according to compressive strength and absorption*

Designation	Class	Average compressive strength not less than N/mm^2	Average absorption (5hrs boiling or vacuum) % by weight not greater than
Engineering	A	69.0	4.5
	B	48.5	7.0
Loadbearing brick	15	103.5	
	10	69.0	
	7	48.5	
	5	34.5	No specific requirement
	4	27.5	
	3	20.5	
	2	14.0	
	1	7.0	

Table 2.4 Compressive strength classes and requirement

Designation	Class	Mean compressive strength of 10 bricks not less than	Shrinkage not greater than
		N/mm^2	
Loadbearing brick	7	48.5	0.040%
	6	41.5	
or	5	34.5	
Facing brick	4	27.5	
	3	20.5	
Facing brick or common brick	2	14.0	

2.2.1 Compressive Strength

From the structural point of view, the compressive strength of the unit is the controlling factor. Bricks of various strengths are available to suit a wide range of architectural and engineering requirements. Table 2.3 gives classification of bricks according to the compressive strength. For low-rise buildings, bricks of 5.2 N/mm^2 should be sufficient. For damp-proof courses low-absorption engineering bricks are usually required.

Calcium silicate bricks of various strengths are also available. Table 2.4 gives the class and strength of these bricks available.

2.2.2 Absorption

Bricks contain pores; some may be 'through' pores, others are 'cul-de-sac' or even sealed and inaccessible. The 'through' pores allow air to escape in the 24 hours absorption test (BS 3921) and permit free passage of water. However, others in a simple immersion test do not allow the passage of water, hence the requirement for a 5 hours boiling or vacuum test. The absorption is the amount of water which is taken up to fill these pores in a brick by displacing the air. The saturation coefficient is the ratio of 24 hours cold absorption to maximum absorption in vacuum or boiling. The absorption of clay bricks varies from 4.5 to 21% by weight and those of calcium silicate from 7 to 21% by weight. The saturation coefficient of bricks may range approximately from 0.2 to 0.88. Neither the absorption nor the saturation coefficient necessarily indicate the liability of bricks to decay by frost or chemical action.

2.2.3 Frost Resistance

The resistance of bricks to frost is very variable and depends on the degree of exposure to driving rain and temperature. Engineering bricks with high compressive strength and low absorption are expected to be frost resistant. However, some bricks of low strength and high absorption may be resistant to frost compared to low-absorption and high-strength brick.

Bricks can only be damaged provided 90% of the available pore space is filled with water about freezing temperature, since water expands one tenth on freezing. Hence, low or high absorption of water by a brick does not signify that all the available pores will become filled with water. Calcium silicate bricks of 14 N/mm^2 or above are weather-resistant.

In the United Kingdom, frost damage is relatively uncommon as brickwork is seldom sufficiently saturated by rain, except in unprotected cornices, parapets and retaining walls. However, bricks and mortar must be carefully selected to avoid damage due to frost. Fig. 2.3 and Table 2.9 show the minimum qualities of clay and calcium silicate bricks to be used for various positions in walls.

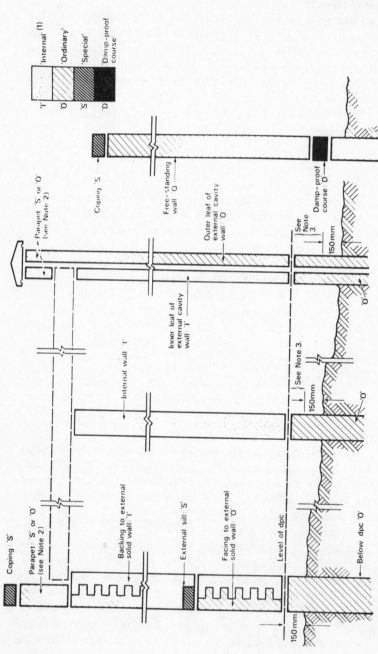

Notes: 1 If there is early frost risk, use 'ordinary' quality. 2 Parapets: rendered on one side only, 'ordinary'; not rendered, 'special' preferred and necessary with early frost risk; rendered on both sides, not desirable but if unavoidable use 'special'. 3 CP 121 considers this zone to be at greater risk and suggests the use of 'special' quality bricks.

Fig. 2.3 — Minimum qualities of clay brick for various positions (Crown Copyright — reproduced with the permission of the Building Research Establishment).

2.2.4 Dimensional Changes

2.2.4.1 *Thermal movement*
All building materials expand or contract with the rise and fall of temperature. Typical values of coefficient of thermal expansion of different materials used in building are given in Table 2.5.

Table 2.5 Coefficient of thermal expansion of various building materials

	per $^\circ$C $\times$ 10^{-6}
Brickwork, clay	5 to 7.0
Brickwork, calcium silicate	14.4
Wood	3.6 to 5.4
Concrete	10 to 14
Steel	11 to 13
Glass	9.0
Aluminium	24.0

2.2.4.2 *Moisture movement*
One of the common causes of cracking and decay of building materials is moisture movement, which may be wholly or partly reversible or, in some circumstances, irreversible. The designer should be aware of the magnitude of this movement.

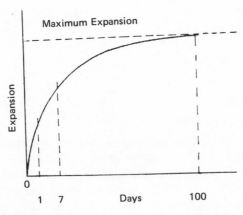

Fig. 2.4 – Expansion of kiln-fresh bricks due to absorption of moisture from atmosphere.

Clay bricks being taken from the kiln expand owing to absorption of water from the atmosphere. The magnitude of this expansion depends on the type of brick and its firing temperature and is wholly irreversible. A large part of this irreversible movement takes place within a few days, as shown in Fig. 2.4, and the rest takes place over a period of about six months. Because of this moisture movement, bricks coming fresh from the kiln should never be delivered straight to the site. Generally, the accepted time lag is a fortnight. Subsequent moisture movement is unlikely to exceed 0.02%.

In addition to this, bricks also undergo partly or wholly reversible expansion or contraction due to wetting or drying. This is not very significant except in the case of the calcium silicate bricks. Hence, the designer should incorporate 'expansion' joints in all walls of any considerable length as a precaution against cracking. Normally, movement joints in calcium silicate brickwork may be provided at intervals of 4.5 to 9.0 m depending upon the moisture content of bricks at the time of laying. In clay brickwork, the expansion joints at intervals of 12.2 to 18.3 m may be provided to accommodate thermal or other movements.

Some indication of reversible or irreversible movement of various building materials is shown in Table 2.6.

Table 2.6 Moisture movement in different building materials

Materials	% Movement	
	Irreversible	Reversible
Clay bricks	0.10 − 0.20 (expansion)	negligible
Calcium silicate	0.001 − 0.05	0.001 − 0.05
Metal and glass	NIL	NIL
Dense concrete and mortar	0.02 − 0.12 (drying shrinkage)	0.01 − 0.055

2.2.5 Soluble Salts

2.2.5.1 *Efflorescence*

All clay bricks contain soluble salts to some extent. The salt can also find its way from mortar or soil or by contamination of brick by foreign agents. In a new building when the brickwork dries out owing to evaporation of water, the dissolved salts normally appear as a white deposit termed 'efflorescence' on the surface of bricks. Sometimes the colour may be yellow or pale green because of presence of vanadium or chromium. The texture may vary from light and fluffy to hard and glassy. Efflorescence is caused by sulphates of sodium, potassium, magnesium and calcium; not all of these may be present in a particular case. Efflorescence can take place on drying out brickwork after construction or subsequently if it is allowed to become very wet. By and large, efflorescence does not normally result in decay, but in the United Kingdom, magnesium sulphate or sodium sulphate do cause disruption due to crystallisation. Abnormal amounts of sodium sulphate, constituting more than 3% by weight of a brick, will cause disruption of its surface.

2.2.5.2 *Sulphate attack*
Sulphates slowly react in presence of water with tri-calcium aluminate, which is one of the constituents of Portland cement, and hydraulic lime. If water containing dissolved sulphate from clay bricks reaches the mortar this reaction takes place, causing mortar to crack and spall and thus resulting in the disintegration of the brickwork. Sulphate attack is only possible if the brickwork is exposed to very long and persistent wet condition. A chimney, parapets, and an earth retaining wall which has not been properly protected from excessive dampness, may be vulnerable to sulphate attack. In general, it is advisable to keep walls as dry as possible. In conditions of severe exposure to rain, special quality bricks or sulphate-resistant cement should be used. The resistance of mortar against sulphate attack can be increased by specifying a fairly rich mix and replacing lime with a plasticiser.

2.2.6 Fire Resistance
Clay bricks are subjected to very much higher temperatures during firing than they are likely to be exposed to in a building fire. As a result, they possess excellent fire resistance properties. Calcium silicate bricks have similar fire resistance properties as clay bricks.

2.3 MORTAR

The second component in brickwork is mortar, which for loadbearing brickwork should be a Cement:Lime:Sand mix in one of the designations shown in Table 2.7. For low-strength bricks a weaker mortar, 1:2:9 mix by volume, may be appropriate.

2.3.1 Function and Requirement of Mortar
In deciding the type of mortar the properties need to be considered are:

i) Development of early strength
ii) Workability, i.e. ability to spread easily
iii) Water retentivity, i.e. the ability of mortar to retain water against the suction of brick. (If water is not retained and is extracted quickly by a high-absorptive brick, there will be insufficient water left in the mortar joint for hydration of the cement, resulting in poor bond between brick and mortar)

Table 2.7 Requirements for mortar (BS 5628)

| Mortar designation | Types of mortar (proportion by volume) | | | Mean compressive strength at 28 days | |
	Cement : lime : sand	Masonry cement : sand	Cement : sand with plasticizer	Preliminary (laboratory) tests	Site tests
				N/mm²	N/mm²
(i)	1 : 0 to ¼ : 3	—	—	16.0	11.0
(ii)	1 : ½ : 4 to 4½	1 : 2½ to 3½	1 : 3 to 4	6.5	4.5
(iii)	1 : 1 : 5 to 6	1 : 4 to 5	1 : 5 to 6	3.6	2.5
(iv)	1 : 2 : 8 to 9	1 : 5½ to 6½	1 : 7 to 8	1.5	1.0

Increasing strength

{ Increasing ability to accommodate movement, e.g. due to settlement, temperature and moisture changes

Increasing resistance to frost attack during construction

Improvement in bond and consequent resistance to rain penetration

Direction of change in properties is shown by the arrows

iv) Proper development of bond with the brick
v) Resistance to cracking and rain penetration
vi) Resistance to frost and chemical attack, e.g. by soluble sulphate
vii) Immediate and long-term appearance.

2.3.2 Cement

The various types of cement used for mortar are:

i) *Portland Cement:* Ordinary and rapid-hardening conforming to a standard such as BS 12. Rapid-hardening cement may be used instead of ordinary Portland cement where higher early strength is required; otherwise its properties are similar.

    Sulphate-resistant cement should be used in situations where the brickwork is expected to remain wet for prolonged periods or where it is susceptible to sulphate attack, e.g. in brickwork in contact with sulphate-bearing soil.

ii) *Masonry Cement:* This is a mixture of approximately 75% ordinary Portland cement, an inert mineral filler, and an air-entraining agent. The mineral filler is used to reduce the cement content, and the air entraining agent is added to improve the workability. Mortar made from masonry cement will have lower strength compared to a normal cement mortar of similar mix. The other properties of the mortar made from the masonry cement is intermediate between cement:lime:sand mortar and plasticised cement:sand mortar.

2.4 LIME: NON-HYDRAULIC OR SEMI-HYDRAULIC LIME

Lime is added to cement mortar to improve the workability, water retention, and bonding properties. The water retentivity property of lime is particularly important in situations where dry bricks might remove a considerable amount of water from the mortar thus leaving less than required for the hydration of the cement. Two types of lime are used: non-hydraulic or semi-hydraulic as one of the constituents of mortar for brickwork. These limes are differentiated on the basis that they harden and develop their strengths. Non-hydraulic lime initially stiffens because of loss of water by evaporation or suction by bricks, and eventually harden because of slow carbonation, i.e. absorption of carbon dioxide from the air to change calcium hydroxide to calcium carbonate. Semi-hydraulic lime will harden in wet conditions. The constitution of hydraulic lime is similar to Portland cement, and hardens owing to chemical reaction with water rather than atmospheric action. In the United Kingdom, the lime used for mortar must conform to BS 890.

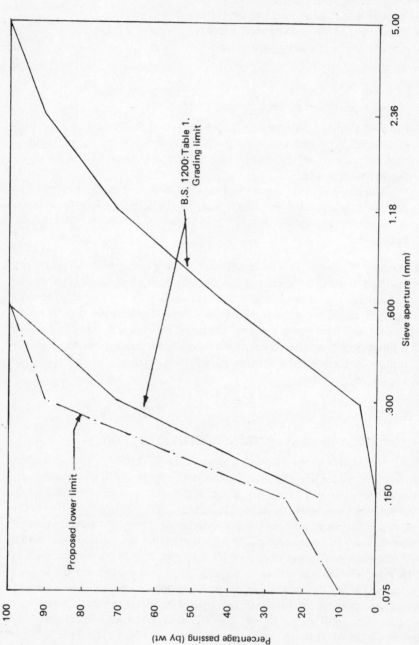

Fig. 2.5 — Proposed grading limits for mortar sand.

2.5 SAND

The sand for mortar must be clean, sharp, and free from salt and organic contamination. Most natural sand contains a small quantity of silt or clay. A small quantity of silt improves the workability. Loam or clay is moisture-sensitive and in large quantities causes shrinkage of mortar. Marine and estuarine sand should not be used unless washed completely to remove magnesium and sodium chloride salts which are deliquescent and attract moisture. Specifications of sand used for mortar, such as BS 1200, prescribe grading limits for the particle size distribution. The limits given in BS 1200 are as shown in Fig. 2.5. Available sand will often be found to lie outside these limits and a survey conducted in Scotland showed that 40% of natural building sands, used successfully in practice, are outside the BS 1200 grading limits. As mortars made from these natural building sands were found to satisfy the strength requirements of BS 5628, it has been suggested that a revised lower limit admitting sands with a higher proportion of fine particles, would be more practical. This is shown in Fig. 2.5.

2.6 WATER

Mixing water for mortar should be clean and free from contaminants either dissolved or in suspension. Ordinary drinking water will be suitable.

2.7 PLASTICISED PORTLAND CEMENT MORTAR

To reduce the cement content and to improve the workability, plasticiser, which entrains air, may be used. Plasticised mortars have poor water retention properties and develop poor bond with highly absorptive bricks. Excessive use of plasticiser will have a detrimental effect on strength, hence manufacturers' instructions must be strictly followed.

2.8 USE OF PIGMENTS

On occasion coloured mortar is required for architectural reasons. Such pigments should be used strictly in accordance with the instructions of the manufacturers since excessive amounts of pigment will reduce the compressive strength of mortar and interface bond strength. The quantity of pigment should not be more than 10% of the weight of the cement. In case of carbon black it should not be more than 3%.

2.9 FROST INHIBITORS

Calcium chloride or preparations based on calcium chloride should not be used, since they attract water and cause dampness in a wall, resulting in corrosion of wall ties and efflorescence.

2.10 PROPORTIONING AND STRENGTH

The constituents of mortar are mixed by volume. The proportions of material and strength is given in Table 2.7. For loadbearing brickwork the mortar must be gauged properly by the use of gauging boxes and preferably should be weigh-batched.

Recent research (Fig. 2.6) has shown that the water/cement ratio is the most important factor which affects the compressive strength of grades I, II and III mortars. In principle, therefore, it would be advisable for the structural engineer to specify the water/cement ratio for mortar to be used for structural

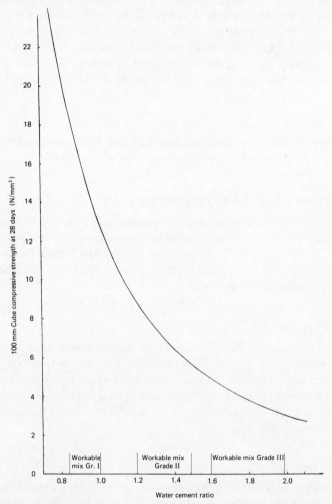

Fig. 2.6 – Effect of water/cement ratio on the compressive strength of mortar of grades I, II and III.

brickwork; but, in practice, the water/cement ratio for a given mix will be determined by workability. There are various laboratory tests for measuring the consistency of mortar, and these have been related to workability. Thus in the United Kingdom, a dropping ball test is used in which an acrylic ball of 10 mm diameter is dropped on to the surface of a sample of mortar from a height of 250 mm. A ball penetration of 10 mm is associated with satisfactory workability. The test is, however, not used on site, and it is generally left to the bricklayer to adjust the water content to achieve optimum workability. This in fact achieves a reasonably consistent water/cement ratio which varies from one mix to another. The water/cement ratio for 10 mm ball penetration, representing satisfactory workability, has been indicated in Fig. 2.6 for the three usual mortar mixes.

It is important that the practice of adding water to partly set mortar to restore workability (known as 'knocking up' the mix) should be prevented.

2.11 CHOICE OF UNIT AND MORTAR

Tables 2.8 and 2.9 show the recommended minimum quality of clay or calcium silicate bricks and mortar grades which should be used in various situations from the point of view of durability.

2.12 WALL TIES

In the United Kingdom, external cavity walls are used for environmental reasons. The two skins of the wall are tied together to provide some degree of interaction. Wall ties for cavity walls should be galvanised mild steel and must comply to BS 1243. Three types of ties (Fig. 2.7) are used for cavity walls.
a)   Vertical twist type made from 20 mm wide, 3.2 to 4.83 mm thick metal strip
b)   'Butterfly' – made from 3.15 mm wire, and
c)   Double-triangle type – made from 4.5 mm wire.

For loadbearing brickwork vertical twist type ties should be used for maximum co-action. For a low-rise building, or a situation where large differential movements is expected or for reason of sound insulation, more flexible ties should be selected. In specially unfavourable situations non-ferrous or stainless steel ties may be required.

Table 2.8 Minimum qualities of bricks and recommended mortar groups (i–v of Table 2.7)
(Taken from *BRE Digest* No. 164)

Constructional element	Early frost hazard (a)			
	no		yes	
	brick	mortar	brick	mortar
Internal walls and inner leaf of cavity walls	Internal	v	ordinary	iii or plasticised iv
Backing to external solid walls	internal	iv	ordinary	iii or plasticised iv
External walls: outer leaf of cavity walls:				
– above damp-proof course	ordinary	iv(c)	ordinary	iii(c)
– below damp-proof course	ordinary	iii(d, g)	ordinary	iii(b, d, g)
Parapet walls: free-standing walls: domestic chimneys:				
– rendered (e)	ordinary	iii(f)	ordinary	iii(f)
– not rendered	special preferred or ordinary	ii iii	special	ii
Sillis and copings: earth-retaining walls backfilled with free-draining material	special	i	special	i

Notes: (a) During construction, before mortar has hardened (say 7 days after laying) or before the wall is protected against the entry of rain at the top. (b) If the bricks are to be laid wet, *see* 'Cold weather bricklaying', *Digest* 160. (c) If to be rendered, lay in mortar not weaker than group iii, preferably with sulphate-resisting cement. (d) If sulphates are present in the groundwater and ordinary quality bricks are used, use sulphate-resisting cement in the mortar. (e) Parapet walls of clay bricks should not be rendered on both sides: if this is unavoidable, select mortar as though *not* rendered. (f) If the presence of sulphates in the bricks is suspected, group iii mortar made with sulphate-resisting cement is preferred. (g) CP 121 considers the zone of brickwork more than 150 mm above ground level and below damp-proof course to be at greater risk and suggests the use of 'special' quality bricks.

Table 2.9 Minimum quality of calcium silicate bricks and mortars for durability

Element of construction		Minimum quality of bricks class (see note 1)	Appropriate mortar designation (see note 2)	
			When there is no risk of frost during construction	When freezing may occur during construction
Inner-leaf of cavity walls and internal walls	unplastered	2	(iv)	(iii)
	plastered	2	(v)	(iii)
Backing to external solid walls		2	(iv)	(iii)
External walls including the outer-leaf of cavity walls and facing to solid construction	above damp-proof course (dpc) near to ground level	2	(iv)	(iii)
	below this dpc but more than 150 mm above finished ground level	2	(iii)	(iii)
	within 150 mm of ground or below ground	3	(iii) (see note 4)	(iii) (see note 4)
External free-standing walls (see note 3)		3	(iii)	(iii)
Parapets	unrendered	3	(iii)	(iii)
	rendered	3	(iv)	(iii)
Sills and copings of bricks		4	(ii)	(ii)
Earth-retaining walls (see note 5)		4	(ii) (see note 3)	(ii) (see note 3)

NOTE 1: The classification of bricks is given in Table 2.4. NOTE 2: The designation of mortars is that given in Table 2.7. The mortar designations shown in this table are those considered most appropriate in relation to durability. Loading requirements (see BS 6528: Part 1) or other special factors may necessitate the use of a type with higher strength. NOTE 3: Where sulphates are present in the ground water, the use of sulphate-resisting cement for the mortar may be necessary. NOTE 4: An effective and continuous dpc should be provided at the top of the wall, as well as just above ground level. NOTE 5: Walls should be backfilled with free-draining materials as recommended in the *Civil Engineering Code of Practice No. 2: Earthretaining Structures*, published by the Institution of Structural Engineers, 1951. This is to be revised by BSI and published as a British Standard.

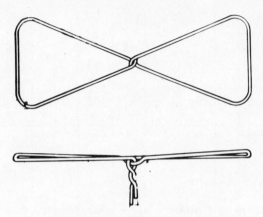

Butterfly type wall ties

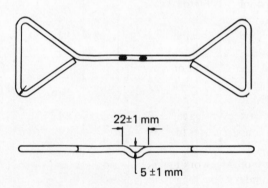

Double triangle type wall tie

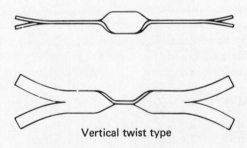

Vertical twist type

Fig. 2.7 — Metal wall ties suitable for cavity walls.

CHAPTER 3

Brick Masonry Properties

3.1 GENERAL

Structural design in brick masonry requires a clear understanding of the behaviour of the composite brick-mortar material under various stress conditions. Primarily, masonry walls are vertical loadbearing elements in which resistance to compressive stress is the predominant factor in design. However, walls are frequently required to resist horizontal shear forces or lateral pressure from wind, and therefore the strength of brickwork in shear and in tension must also be considered.

Current design values for the strength of brickwork in compression, tension and shear have been derived on an empirical basis as a result of tests on piers, walls and smaller specimens. Whilst this has resulted in safe designs, it provides very little insight into the behaviour of the material under stress, and in recent years attempts have been made to establish theories of failure for brickwork in direct compression and under biaxial stress resulting from combined compression and shear.

The strength of brickwork in direct tension is usually discounted in structural design, but flexural tensile strength is of importance in relation to brickwork panels which are loaded mainly by lateral pressure. In many cases such panels are subjected to biaxial bending, and the orthotropic nature of brickwork properties has to be considered. Specifically, the different flexural tensile strengths parallel to and at right angles to the bed joints must be known.

The stress-strain relationship of brick masonry does not usually enter directly into design calculations for loadbearing walls, but in some rather exceptional cases it may be necessary to consider deformation of structures, and thus knowledge of elastic moduli will be required. This will also arise when composite action between brickwork and steel or concrete members is a factor in design.

3.2 COMPRESSIVE STRENGTH

3.2.1 Indications from Standard Tests

A number of important points have been derived from compression tests on brickwork and associated standard materials tests. These include, firstly, the observation that brickwork loaded in uniform compression usually fails by the

development of tension cracks parallel to the axis of loading, that is as a result of tensile stresses at right angles to the primary compression, as shown in Fig. 3.1. This fact has been well known since the early years of brickwork testing. Secondly, it is evident that the strength of brickwork in compression is much smaller than the nominal compressive strength of the bricks from which it is built, as given by a standard compression test. On the other hand, brickwork strength may greatly exceed the cube crushing strength of the mortar used in it. Finally, it has been shown that the compressive strength of brickwork varies, roughly, as the square root of the nominal brick crushing strength and as the third or fourth root of the mortar cube strength.

From these observations it has been inferred (1) that the secondary tensile stresses which cause splitting failure of the brickwork result from the restrained deformation of the mortar in the bed joints of the brickwork; (2) that the apparent compressive strength of bricks in a standard crushing test is not a direct measure of the strength of the unit in brickwork, since the mode of failure is different in the two situations; and (3) that mortar is able to withstand higher compressive stresses in a brickwork bed joint because of the biaxial or triaxial nature of the stressing in this situation.

3.2.2 The Interaction of Brick and Bed Material

It is possible to detect a paradox in the evidence from normal brickwork testing summarised above, namely, that whilst the cube crushing strength of mortar is only weakly related to brickwork strength by a third or fourth root relationship, nevertheless the mortar exerts a controlling influence on the brickwork strength achieved.

This has been demonstrated in experiments in which brickwork prisms consisting of loose bricks, the bedding planes of which were ground flat, achieved compressive strengths approximately twice as high as those obtained from prisms with normal mortar joints. In another set of experiments, the bed material in a number of model brick prisms was varied from rubber at one extreme to steel at the other. The results, summarised in Table 3.1 show that there is an eightfold change in the prism strength with the substitution of steel for rubber in the bed joints. In the case of rubber jointing material, the bricks failed in tension as a result of tensile stress induced by the deformation of the rubber. Steel in the bed joints, on the other hand, had the effect of restraining lateral deformation of the bricks, and this induced a state of biaxial compressive stress in them. Failure in this case was by crushing, as in a typical compression test. Mortar has properties intermediate between these extremes, causing splitting rather than crushing failure of the bricks.

Fig. 3.1 *opposite* – Typical compressive failure of a brick masonry wall by development of tensile cracks parallel to the axis of loading.

Table 3.1 Effect of different joint materials on the compressive strength
of 3-brick prisms. Brick faces ground flat: six specimens of each
type tested

Joint material	Compressive strength (N/mm^2)
Steel	56.6
Plywood	46.4
Hardboard	43.9
Polythene	17.0
Rubber with fibres	11.70
Soft rubber	7.0
No joint material	37.2

3.2.3 Formulae for Brickwork Strength based on Elastic Analysis

Consideration of the qualitative evidence such as discussed in the preceding
paragraphs has suggested that fomulae for brickwork strength in compression,
based on an elastic analysis of the brick-mortar complex, could be derived.

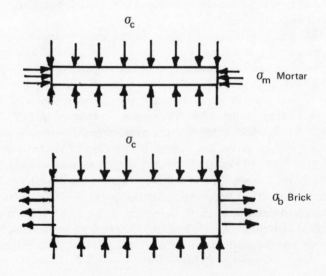

Fig. 3.2– Elastic theory of failure of brickwork.

Thus, referring to Fig. 3.2, and considering horizontal strains:

$$\text{Strain in mortar: } \epsilon_m = -\frac{\sigma_m}{E_m} + \nu_m \cdot \frac{\sigma_c}{E_m} \qquad (3.1)$$

$$\text{Strain in brick: } \epsilon_b = \frac{\sigma_b}{E_b} + \nu_b \cdot \frac{\sigma_c}{E_b} \qquad (3.2)$$

where E_m, E_b, ν_b are respectively the elastic moduli and Poisson's ratios for mortar and brick as denoted by the subscripts.

The lateral strains in mortar and brick are assumed to be uniform and equal. Furthermore, from statical equilibrium considerations, the total lateral forces in mortar and brick are equal and opposite. Hence

$$\sigma_m = d/t \cdot \sigma_b = r \cdot \sigma_b$$

where d = depth of brick and t = thickness of mortar joint. Equating (3.1) and (3.2) and rearranging terms gives:

$$\sigma_b \left(\frac{1}{E_b} + \frac{r}{E_m} \right) = \sigma_c \left(\frac{\nu_m}{E_m} - \frac{\nu_b}{E_b} \right) \quad .$$

And putting $E_b/E_m = m$

$$\sigma_b = \left(\frac{\nu_m \cdot m - \nu_b}{1 + r \cdot m} \right) \sigma_c \quad . \qquad (3.3)$$

At this point it is necessary to introduce a failure criterion for the brick material which may be taken as a limiting tensile strain. This will be:

$$\epsilon_{ult} = \frac{\sigma_b}{E_b} + \nu_b \cdot \frac{\sigma_c}{E_b} \qquad (3.4)$$

or, putting $\sigma'_b = E_b \cdot \epsilon_{ult}$,

$$\sigma_b = \sigma'_b - \nu_b \cdot \sigma_c \quad .$$

The term σ_b' is the stress corresponding to tensile failure of the brick. Substituting in (3.3) and rearranging, the limiting compressive stress is:

$$\sigma_c = \frac{\sigma_b{'}}{\dfrac{\nu_b + \nu_m \cdot m - \nu_b}{1 + r \cdot m}} \; . \tag{3.5}$$

The difficulty with this approach to brickwork strength lies in the fact that the materials, particularly the mortar, are not elastic up to the point of failure and therefore the values of Young's modulus and Poisson's ratio for the two components of the system cannot be uniquely defined. It is possible that a nonlinear analysis might be produced, but it would be difficult to determine the necessary deformation characteristics experimentally. Notwithstanding this limitation, fair agreement has been demonstrated with experimental results, and formulae derived in this way do give an indication of some of the factors controlling brickwork strength. Thus, it is clear that the ratio of joint thickness to brick depth is such a factor and is of practical importance in relation to workmanship since the effect of over-thick joints is to reduce the strength of the brickwork. This effect is illustrated in Fig. 3.3.

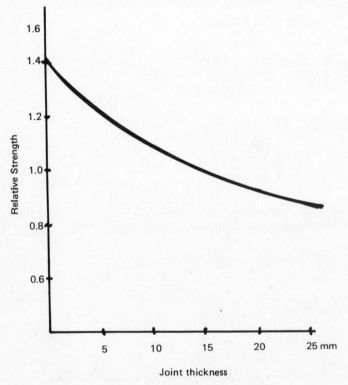

Fig. 3.3 – Effect of joint thickness on brickwork strength.

3.2.4 Failure Criterion Based on Biaxial Strength of Bricks and Mortar

An alternative approach to the definition of brickwork strength is based on consideration of the biaxial or triaxial strength of the component materials. For any given brick material, it is possible to determine an envelope curve defining the combination of vertical compressive and horizontal tensile stresses which will lead to failure. This will typically be as shown in Fig. 3.4, curve 'A'. It is also possible to determine a corresponding relationship for mortar, which will be in a state of triaxial compression. Tests show this to be almost linear, with an intercept on the axis of major principal stress corresponding to the uniaxial compressive strength of the material. Assuming that the lateral stresses in both brick and mortar are uniform through each component, it is possible to define the strength of the masonry by superimposing the mortar strength curve ('B' in Fig. 3.4) on the brick strength curve, having first multiplied the lateral compressive stresses in the mortar by the ratio of the mortar bed thickness to the brick thickness. This is necessary in order to satisfy the statical condition that the total compression in the mortar is equal to the total tension in the brick. This superposition is indicated in Fig. 3.4, and the point of intersection of 'A' and 'B' defines the compressive strength of the particular brick–mortar combination.

It will be evident from consideration of Fig. 3.4 that mortar strength and the ratio of joint thickness to brick thickness are determining factors in respect of masonry strength for a given brick. The strength characteristics of the mortar will in turn depend on its composition and on the nature of its constituents, as explained in Chapter 2.

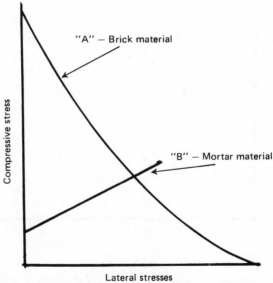

Fig. 3.4 – Stress failure theory.

3.2.5 Experimental Measurement of Brick Masonry Compressive Strength

The preceding paragraphs are intended to give some indication of the internal behaviour of brick masonry under compressive stress. In structural design, the basic problem is to select a brick–mortar combination the strength of which will be sufficient to resist the imposed loads. In practice, the necessary information is obtained from either *ad hoc* tests on samples of masonry or, more usually tables which collate experimentally determined brickwork strengths with brick compressive strengths and mortar mixes or 'cube' strengths. The material strengths

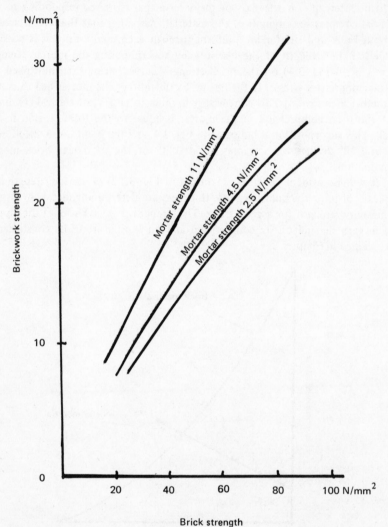

Fig. 3.5 – Relationship between brick crushing strength and brickwork strength for various mortar strengths. Based on test results.

must be determined by the same standard procedures as used in the preparation of the tables, as variations in test methods can produce quite different results for nominally the same property. Such tables of masonry strength will assume a normal joint thickness of about 10 mm and will be valid only for specified types of bricks. These various conditions and qualifications account for the apparent differences which exist between masonry strengths shown in national codes of practice for seemingly the same component material strength.

Fig. 3.5 illustrates the typical empirical relationship between brick strength and brickwork strength for three different mortar cube strengths. In general, brickwork strength is in the region of 0.3 to 0.4 of the brick strength and is not very sensitive to mortar strength .

The curves shown in Fig. 3.5 are similar to those which can be derived from the more fundamental considerations discussed in section 3.2.4.

3.3 STRENGTH OF BRICKWORK IN COMBINED SHEAR AND COMPRESSION

The strength of brickwork in combined shear and compression is of importance in relation to the resistance of buildings to lateral forces. Many tests on brickwork panels subjected to this type of loading have been carried out with a view to establishing limiting stresses for use in design. The results of a large number of tests of this kind are summarised in Fig. 3.6. It is found that there is a 'Coulomb' type of relationship between shear strength and precompression, i.e. there is an initial shear strength dependent on adhesion between the bricks and mortar augmented by a frictional component proportional to the precompression. This may be expressed by the formula

$$\tau = \tau_0 + \mu.\sigma_c \qquad (3.6)$$

where τ_0 = shear strength at zero precompression

μ = an apparent friction coefficient

σ_c = vertical compression stress

This relationship holds for values of compression stress up to levels in excess of 2.0 N/mm^2 for clay bricks, but eventually the ultimate shear stress must be less than the value given by this formula. In the limit, when the compressive stress approaches the crushing strength of the brickwork, the shear resistance will fall to zero.

The shear strength depends on the mortar stength, and for brickwork built with clay bricks of crushing strength between 20 and 50 N/mm^2 the value of τ_0 will be approximately 0.3N/mm^2 for strong (1:¼:3) mortar and 0.2 for medium strength (1:1:6) mortar. The average value of μ is 0.4. Double-frogged or perforated bricks will give higher strengths at low precompressions on account of the mechanical key established between bricks and mortar.

The shear stresses quoted above are average values for walls whose height to length ratio is 1.0 or more, and the strength of a wall is calculated on the plan area of the wall in the plane of the shear force. That is to say, if a wall has returns at right angles to the direction of the shear force, the area of the returns is neglected in calculating the shear resistance of the wall.

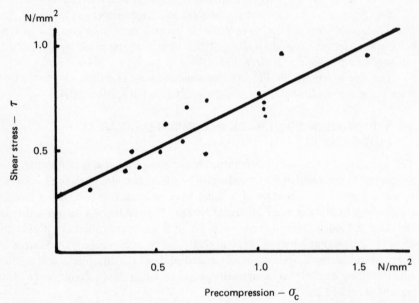

Fig. 3.6 – Typical relationship between shear strength of brickwork and vertical precompression from test results.

3.4 STRENGTH OF BRICKWORK SUBJECT TO BIAXIAL STRESS

3.4.1 Brickwork Subject to Biaxial Stresses

A shear wall resisting a combination of vertical and horizontal forces is an example of a situation in which brickwork is subjected to a biaxial stress condition. In this case, the principal stresses in the masonry will vary in magnitude and direction from one point to another, and failure will be initiated at whatever point the stress condition first becomes critical. In this case the major principal stress will generally be compressive and the minor principal stress tensile.

Other situations in which brickwork is subject to biaxial stress include areas in the vicinity of concentrated loads and in composite wall beam elements.

Although it is not normally necessary to calculate the principal stresses in brickwork for design purposes, an understanding of the failure criteria under complex stresses is valuable.

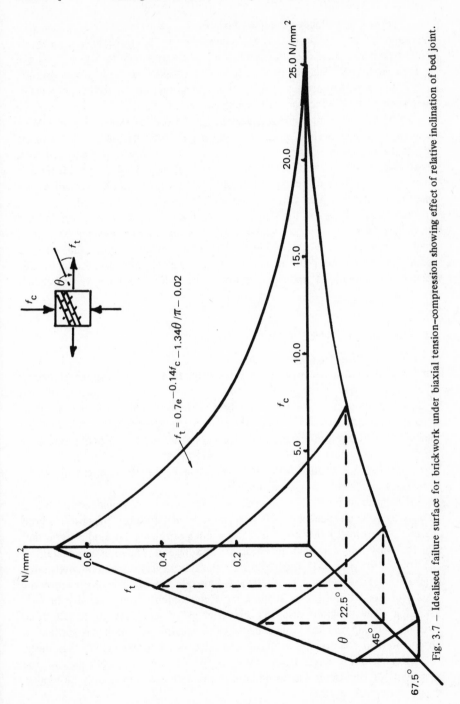

$$f_t = 0.7e^{-0.14f_c} - 1.34\theta/\pi - 0.02$$

Fig. 3.7 – Idealised failure surface for brickwork under biaxial tension-compression showing effect of relative inclination of bed joint.

3.4.2 Failure Criteria under Complex Stresses

Experimental and theoretical studies have shown that the failure criteria for brickwork under biaxial compression-tension are as shown in Fig. 3.7. As will be seen from this diagram, it is necessary to consider not only the magnitude of the two principal stresses but also their inclination relative to the bed joint of the masonry. This is because the strength properties of brickwork are anisotropic.

To apply the failure criterion defined by the surface shown in Fig. 3.7, for example to a shear wall, it would be necessary to calculate the principal stresses at a sufficient number of points in the wall and to compare the result at each point with the failure surface. An accurate calculation is complicated if there is cracking at the base of the wall but, if this does not arise, a standard elastic analysis is sufficient and critical areas are readily identified. Strictly speaking, this procedure will reveal the point and load level at which the first crack takes place. Overall failures of the wall will only occur at some higher load, and to trace the development of cracking up to failure would require the use of a special finite element program which would simulate crack formation by disconnecting elements at node points where the failure criterion was exceeded.

3.5 THE TENSILE STRENGTH OF BRICKWORK

3.5.1 Direct Tensile Strength

Direct tensile stresses can arise in brickwork as a result of in-plane loading effects. These may be caused by wind, by eccentric gravity loads, by thermal or moisture movements or by foundation movement. The tensile resistance of brickwork, particularly across bed joints, is low and variable and therefore is not generally relied upon in structural design. Nevertheless, it is essential that there should be some adhesion between bricks and mortar, and it is necessary to be aware of those conditions which are conducive to the development of mortar bond on which tensile resistance depends.

The mechanism of brick–mortar adhesion is not fully understood but is known to be a physical-chemical process in which the pore structure of both materials is critical. It is known that the grading of the mortar sand is important and that very fine sands are unfavourable to adhesion. The moisture content of the brick at the time of laying is also important: both very dry and fully saturated bricks lead to low bond strength. This is illustrated in Fig. 3.8 which shows the results of bond tensile tests at brick moisture contents from oven-dry to fully saturated. This diagram also indicates the great variability of tensile bond strength and suggests that this is likely to be greatest at a moisture content of about three quarters of full saturation, at least for the bricks used in these tests.

Direct tensile strength of brickwork is typically about 0.4 N/mm^2, but the variability of this figure has to be kept in mind, and it should only be used in design with great caution.

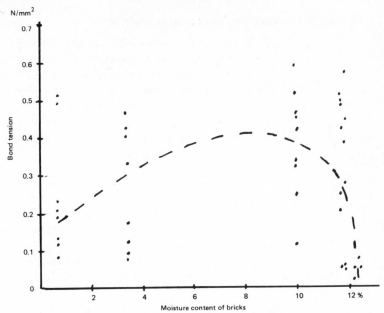

Fig. 3.8 — Variation of brick–mortar adhesion with moisture content of bricks at time of laying.

3.5.2 Flexural Tensile Strength

Brickwork panels used essentially as cladding for buildings have to withstand lateral wind pressure and suction. Some stability is derived from the self weight of a wall, but generally this is insufficient to provide the necessary resistance to wind forces, and therefore reliance has to be placed on the flexural tensile strength of the masonry.

The same factors as influence direct tensile bond, discussed in the preceding section, apply to the development of flexural tensile strength. If a wall is supported only at its base and top, its lateral resistance will depend on the flexural tensile strength developed across the bed joints. If it is supported also on its vertical edges, lateral resistance will depend also on the flexural strength of the brickwork in the direction at right angles to the bed joints. The strength in this direction is typically about three times as great as across the bed joints. If the brick–mortar adhesion is good, the bending strength parallel to the bed joint direction will be limited by the flexural tensile strength of the bricks. If the adhesion is poor, this strength will be limited mainly by the shear strength of the brick-mortar interface in the bed joints.

The flexural tensile strength of clay brickwork ranges from about 2.0 to 0.8 N/mm^2 in the stronger direction, the strength in bending across the bed joints being about one third of this. As in the case of direct tension, the strength developed is dependent on the absorption characteristics of the bricks and also on the type of mortar used.

3.6 STRESS-STRAIN PROPERTIES OF BRICKWORK

Brick masonry is generally treated as a linearly elastic material, although tests
indicate that the stress–strain relationship is approximately parabolic, as shown
in Fig. 3.9. Under service conditions brickwork is stressed only up to a fraction
of its ultimate load, and therefore the assumption of a linear stress–strain curve
is acceptable for the calculation of normal structural deformations.

Various formulae have been suggested for the determination of Young's
modulus. This parameter is, however, rather variable even for nominally identical
specimens, and as an approximation, it may be assumed that:

$$E = 700\sigma_c^1 \tag{3.7}$$

where σ_c^1 is the crushing strength of the masonry. This value will apply up to
about 75% of the ultimate strength.

For estimating long-term deformations a reduced value of E should be used,
in the region of one half to one third of that given by equation (3.7).

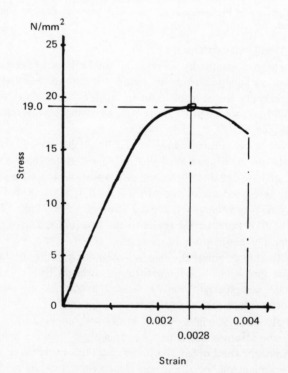

Fig. 3.9 — Typical stress-strain curve for brick masonry.

3.7 EFFECTS OF WORKMANSHIP ON BRICKWORK STRENGTH

Brickwork has a very long tradition of building by craftsmen, without engineering supervision of the kind applied to reinforced concrete construction. Consequently, it is frequently regarded with some suspicion as a structural material and carries very much higher safety factors than concrete. There is of course some justification for this, in that, if supervision is non-existent, any structural element, whether of brickwork or concrete, will be of uncertain strength. If, on the other hand, the same level of supervision is applied to brickwork as is customarily required for concrete, brickwork will be quite as reliable as concrete. It is therefore important for engineers designing and constructing in brick masonry to have an appreciation of the workmanship factors which are significant in developing a specified strength. This information has been obtained by carrying out tests on walls which have had known defects built into them and comparing the results with corresponding tests on walls without defects.

The most common workmanship defects may be summarised as follows:

(a) *Failure to fill bed-joints:* It is essential that the bed joints in brickwork should be completely filled. Gaps in the mortar bed can result simply from carelessness or haste or from a practice known as 'furrowing' which means that the bricklayer makes a gap with his trowel in the middle of the mortar bed parallel to the face of the wall. Tests show that imcompletely filled bed joints can reduce the strength of brickwork by as much as 33%.

Failure to fill the vertical joints has been found to have very little effect on the compressive strength of brickwork but does reduce the flexural resistance. Also, unfilled perpend joints are undesirable from the point of view of weather exclusion and sound insulation as well as being indicative of careless workmanship generally.

(b) *Bed Joints of Excessive Thickness:* It was pointed out in discussing the compressive strength of brickwork that increase in joint thickness has the effect of reducing masonry strength because it generates higher lateral tensile stresses in the bricks than would be the case with thin joints. Thus, bed joints of 16 – 19 mm thickness will result in a reduction of compressive strength of up to 30% as compared with 10 mm thick joints.

(c) *Deviation from Verticality or Alignment:* A wall which is built out of plumb, which is bowed or which is out of alignment with the wall in the storey above or below, will give rise to eccentric loading and consequent reduction in strength. Thus a wall containing a defect of this type of 12 – 20 mm will be some 13 – 15% weaker than one which does not.

(d) *Exposure to Adverse Weather after Laying:* Newly laid brickwork should be protected from excessive heat or freezing conditions until the mortar has been cured. Excessive loss of moisture by evaporation or exposure to hot weather may prevent complete hydration of the cement and consequent failure to develop the normal strength of the mortar. The strength of a wall may be reduced by 10% as a result. Freezing can cause displacement of a wall from the vertical with corresponding reduction in strength. Proper curing can be achieved by covering the work with polythene sheets, and in cold weather it may also be necessary to heat the materials if bricklaying has to be carried out in freezing conditions.

(e) *Failure to Adjust Suction of Bricks:* A rather more subtle defect can arise if slender walls have to be built using highly absorptive bricks. The reason for this is illustrated in Fig. 3.10 which suggests how a bed joint may become 'pillow' shaped if the bricks above it are slightly rocked as they are laid. If water has been removed from the mortar by the suction of the bricks, it may have become too dry for it to recover its originally flat shape. The resulting wall will obviously lack stability as a result of the convex shape of the mortar bed and maybe as much as 50% weaker than would be expected from consideration of the brick strength and mortar mix. The remedy is to wet the bricks before laying so as to reduce their suction rate below $2kg/m^2/min$, and a proportion of lime in the mortar mix will help to retain water in it against the suction of the bricks.

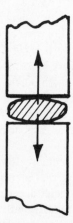

Fig. 3.10 – Effect of moisture absorption from mortar bed. Movement of bricks after laying results in 'pillow' shaped mortar bed.

In practice, these defects will be present to some extent and, in unsatisfactory work, a combination of them could result in a wall being only half as strong in compression as it should be. Such a wall, however, would be obviously badly built and would be so far outside any reasonable specification as to be quite unacceptable.

It is, of course, very much better for brickwork to be properly built in the first instance, and time spent by the engineer explaining the importance of the points outlined above to the bricklayer and his immediate supervisor will be time well spent.

CHAPTER 4

A Code of Practice for
Loadbearing Brickwork: BS 5628

4.1 CODES OF PRACTICE : GENERAL

A structural code of practice or standard for brick masonry brings together essential data on which to base the design of structures in this medium. It contains recommendations for dealing with various aspects of design based on what is generally considered to be good practice at the time of preparing the code. Such a document is not, however, a textbook and does not relieve the designer from the responsibility of acquiring a full understanding of the materials used and of the problems of structural action which are implicit in his design. It follows therefore that, in order to use a code of practice satisfactorily, and perhaps even safely, the engineer must make a careful study of its provisions and, as far as possible, their underlying intention. It is not always easy to do this, as codes are written in terms which often conceal the uncertainties of the drafters, and they are seldom accompanied by commentaries which define the basis and limitations of the various clauses.

This chapter is devoted to a general discussion of the British Code of Practice, BS 5628: Part 1: 1978, which deals with unreinforced masonry. Other national codes are generally similar in content although differing considerably in detail. If the reader has to deal with a code other than BS 5628 he may nevertheless find it profitable to make a study of the British code and then make a comparative analysis of the document which he is going to use for his designs.

The provisions of BS 5628 and their application for design will be discussed in detail in subsequent chapters of this book.

4.2 THE BASIS AND STRUCTURE OF BS 5628

The British code is based on limit state principles, superseding CP 111 (1970) which is in permissible stress terms.

The code is arranged in the following five sections:

Section one   :   General: scope, references, symbols etc.

Section two   :   Materials, components and workmanship

Section three   :   Design: objectives and general recommendations

Section four   :   Design: detailed considerations

Section five   :   Design accidental damage.

There are also four appendices which are not technically part of the code but give additional information on various matters.

4.2.1 Section 1: General

The code covers all forms of masonry including brickwork, blockwork, and stone. It is to be noted that the code is based on the assumption that the structural design is to be carried out by a chartered civil or structural engineer or other appropriately qualified person and that the supervision is by suitably qualified persons, although the latter may not always be chartered engineers.

If materials and methods are used that are not referred to by the code such materials and methods are not ruled out, provided that they achieve the standard of strength and durability required by the code and that they are justified by test.

4.2.2 Section 2: Materials, components, symbols etc.

This section deals with materials, components, and workmanship. In general, these should be in accordance with the relevant British Standard (e.g. CP 121 : *Brickwork and blockwork* and BS 5390: *Stone masonry*). Structural units and other masonry materials and components are covered by British Standards, but if used in an unusual way, e.g. bricks laid on stretcher side or on end, appropriate strength tests have to be carried out.

A table in this section (see Table 2.7, p. 30) sets out requirements for mortar in terms of proportion by volume together with indicative compressive strengths at 28 days for preliminary and site tests. The wording of the paragraph referring to this table seems to suggest that both the mix and the strength requirements have to be satisfied simultaneously — this may give rise to some difficulty as variations in sand grading may require adjustment of the mix to obtain the specified strength. Four mortar mixes are suggested, as previously noted, in terms of volumetric proportion. Grades (i), (ii) and (iii) are the most usual for engineered brickwork. Lower-strength mortars may be more appropriate for concrete blockwork where the unit strength is generally lower and shrinkage and moisture movements greater. Mortar additives, other than calcium chloride, are not ruled out but have to be used with care.

In using different materials in combination, e.g. clay bricks and concrete blocks, it is necessary to exercise considerable care to allow differential movements to take place. Thus the code suggests that more flexible wall ties may be substituted for the normal vertical twist ties in cavity walls in which one leaf is built in brickwork and the other in blockwork.

4.2.3 Sections 3 and 4: Design

Sections 3 and 4 contain the main design information, starting with a statement of the basis of design. Unlike its predecessor, CP 111, BS 5628 is based on limit state principles.

It is stated that the primary objective in designing loadbearing masonry members is to ensure an adequate margin of safety against the attainment of the ultimate limit state. In general terms this is achieved by ensuring that

$$\text{Design strength} \geqslant \text{Design load} \quad .$$

As stated in Chapter 1, the terms *design load* and *design strength* are defined as follows:

$$\text{Design load} = \text{characteristic load} \times \gamma_f$$

where γ_f is a partial safety factor introduced to allow for

(a) possible unusual increases in load beyond these considered in deriving the characteristic load,

(b) inaccurate assessment of effects of loading and unforeseen stress redistribution within the structure,

(c) variations in dimensional accuracy achieved in construction.

As a matter of convenience, the γ_f values have (see Table 4.2) been taken in this code to be, with minor differences, the same as in the British code for structural concrete, CP 110: 1971. The effects allowed for by (b) and (c) above may or may not be the same for brickwork and concrete. For example, structural analysis methods normally used for the design of concrete structures are considerably more refined than those used for masonry structures. Dimensional accuracy is related to the degree of supervision applied to site construction which is again normally better for concrete than for masonry. There is, however, no reason why more accurate design methods and better site supervision should not be applied to brickwork construction, and as will be seen presently the latter is taken into account in BS 5628 but by adjusting the material partial safety factor γ_m rather than γ_f.

As explained in Chapter 1, characteristic loads are defined theoretically as those which will not be exceeded in 95% of instances of their application, but as the information necessary to define loads on a statistical basis is seldom available, conventional values are adopted from relevant codes of practice, in the present case from the British Standard Codes of Practice CP 3 Chapter V.

Different values of γ_f are associated with the various loading cases. Reduced values are specified for accidental damage.

Table 4.1 Partial Safety Factors in BS 5628

A – Partial Safety Factors for Loads (γ_f)

(a) *Dead and imposed load*
  design dead load　　　= $0.9G_k$ or $1.4G_k$
  design imposed load　= $1.6Q_k$

(b) *Dead and wind load*
  design dead load　　　= $0.9G_k$ or $1.4G_k$
  design wind load　　　= $1.4W_k$ or $0.015G_k$ whichever is the larger

In the particular case of freestanding walls and laterally loaded wall panels, whose removal would in no way affect the stability of the remaining structure, γ_f applied on the wind load may be taken as 1.2.

(c) *Dead, imposed and wind load*
  design dead load　　　= $1.2G_k$
  design imposed load　= $1.2Q_k$
  design wind load　　　= $1.2W_k$ or $0.015G_k$ whichever is the larger

(d) *Accidental damage*
  design dead load　　　= $0.95G_k$ or $1.05G_k$
  design imposed load　= $0.35Q_k$ except that, in the case of buildings used predominantly for storage, or where the imposed load is of a permanent nature, $1.05Q_k$ should be used
  design wind load　　　= $0.35W_k$
where
  G_k is the characteristic dead load,
  Q_k is the characteristic imposed load,
  W_k is the characteristic wind load,
  and the numerical values are the appropriate γ_f factors.

B – Partial Safety Factors for Materials (γ_m)

		Category of Construction Control:	
		Special	*Normal*
Category of manufacturing	Special	2.5	3.1
control	Normal	2.8	3.5

Turning now to the other side of the limit state equation, *Design strength* is defined as:

$$\text{Characteristic strength}/\gamma_m$$

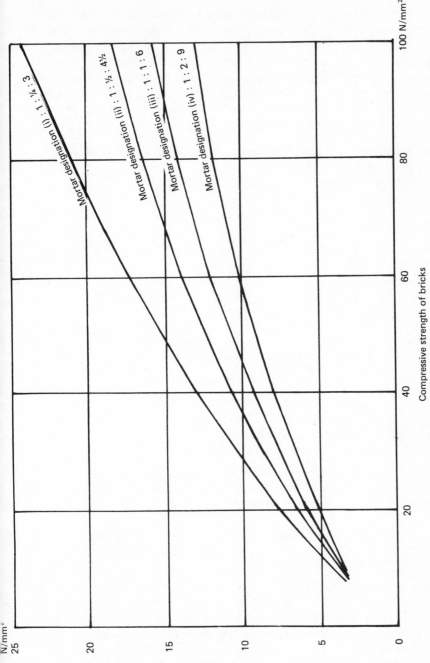

Fig. 4.1 – Characteristic strength of brickwork.

Charactersistic strength is again defined statistically as the strength to be expected in 95% of tests on samples of the material being used. There are greater possibilities of determining characteristic strengths on a statistical basis as compared with loads, but again for convenience, conventional values for characteristic compressive strength are adopted in BS 5628, in terms of brick strength and mortar strength. This information is presented graphically in Fig. 4.1. Similarly, characteristic flexural and shear strengths are from test results but not on a strictly statistical basis. These are shown in Table 4.2.

Table 4.2 Flexural and Shear Characteristic Strengths in BS 5628 (1978)

A – Flexural Charactersitic Strengths for Clay Brickwork

Mortar designation	Plane of failure parallel to bed joints			Plane of failure perpendicular to bed joints		
	(i)	(ii) and (iii)	(iv)	(i)	(ii) and (iii)	(iv)
Clay bricks having a water absorption less than 7%	0.7	0.5	0.4	2.0	1.5	1.2
between 7% and 12%	0.5	0.4	0.35	1.5	1.1	1.0
over 12%	0.4	0.3	0.25	1.1	0.9	0.8

B – Characteristic Shear Strengths

Brickwork built in mortar designation (i), (ii) or (iii):
$f_v = 0.35 + 0.6g_A$ but not exceeding 1.75 N/mm^2

Brickwork built in mortar designation (iv):
$f_v = 0.15 + 0.6g_A$ but not exceeding 1.4 N/mm^2

g_A is the design vertical load per unit area of wall cross-section due to the vertical loads calculated from the appropriate loading contition.

Values of the material partial safety factor γ_m were established by the Code Drafting Committee. In theory this could have been done by statistical calculations – if the relevant parameters for loads and materials had been known and the desired level of safety (i.e. acceptable probability of failure) had been specified. However, these quantities were not known and the first approach to the problem was to try to arrive at a situation whereby the new code would, in a given case, give walls of the same thickness and material strength as the old CP 111. The most obvious procedure was therefore to split the global safety factor of about 5 implied in CP 111 into partial safety factors relating to loads (γ_f) and material strength (γ_m). As the γ_f values were taken from CP 110 this would seem to be a fairly straightforward procedure. However, the situation is more complicated than this – for example, there are different partial safety factors for different categories of load effect; and in limit state design, partial safety factors are applied to characteristic strengths which do not exist in the permissible stress code. Thus more detailed consideration was necessary, and reference was made to the theoretical evaluation of safety factors by statistical analysis. These calculations did not lead directly to the values given in the code but they provided a reference framework whereby the γ_m values selected could be checked. Thus, it was verified that the proposed values were consistent with realistic estimates of variability of materials and that the highest and lowest values of γ_m applying, respectively, to unsupervised and closely supervised work, should result in about the same level of safety. It should be emphasised that, although a considerable degree of judgement went into the selection of the γ_m values, they are not entirely arbitrary and reflect what is known from literally thousands of tests on masonry walls.

The values arrived at are set out in Table 4 of the Code and are shown in Table 4.2.

There are other partial safety factors for *shear* and for *ties*. For *accidental damage* the relevant γ_m values are halved.

It was considered reasonable that the principal partial safety factors for materials in compression should be graded to take into account differences in manufacturing control of bricks and of site supervision. There is therefore a benefit of about 10% for using bricks satisfying the requirement of 'Special' category of manufacture and of about 20% for meeting this category of construction control. The effect of adopting both measures is to reduce γ_m by approximately 30%, i.e. from 3.5 to 2.5.

The requirements for 'Special' category of manufacturing control are quite specific and are set out in the Code. The definition of 'Special' category of construction control is rather more difficult to define, but it is stated in Section One of the code that "the execution of the work is carried out under the direction of appropriately qualified supervisors", and in Section Two that "......workmanship used in the construction of loadbearing walls should comply with the appropriate clause in CP 121 : Part 1....". Taken together these provisions must be met for 'Normal category' of construction control. 'Special category' includes these requirements and in addition requires that the designer should ensure that the work in fact conforms to them and to any additional requirements which he may prescribe. The Code also calls for compressive strength tests on the mortar to be used in order to meet the requirements of 'Special' category of construction control.

A very important paragraph at the beginning of Section 3 of BS 5628 draws attention to the responsibility of the designer to ensure overall stability of the structure, as discussed in Chapter 1 of this book. General considerations of stability are reinforced by the requirement that the structure should be able to resist at any level a horizontal force equal to 1.5% of the characteristic dead load of the structure above the level considered. The danger of divided responsibility for stability is pointed out. Accidents very often result from divided design responsibilities: in one well known case, a large steel building structure collapsed as a result of the main frames having been designed by a consulting engineer and the connections by the steelwork contractor concerned – neither gave proper consideration to the overall stability. Something similar could conceivably happen in a masonry structure if design responsibility for the floors and walls was divided.

The possible effect of accidental damage must also be taken into account in a general way at this stage, although more detailed consideration must be given to this matter as a check on the final design.

Finally, attention is directed to the possible need for temporary supports to walls during construction.

Section 4 is the longest part of the code and provides the data necessary for the design of walls and columns in addition to characteristic strength of materials and partial safety factors.

The basic design of compression members is carried out by calculating their design strength from the formula

$$\frac{\beta \, b.t.f_k}{\gamma_m} \tag{4.1}$$

where β = capacity reduction factor for slenderness and eccentricity

b,t = respectively, width and thickness of the member

f_k = characteristic compressive strength

γ_m = material partial safety factor   .

The capacity reduction factor β has been derived on the assumption that there is a load eccentricity varying from e_x at the top of the wall to zero at the bottom together with an additional eccentricity arising from the lateral deflection related to slenderness. This is neglected if the slenderness ratio (i.e. ratio of effective height to thickness) is less than 6. The additional eccentricity is further assumed to vary from zero at the top and bottom of the wall to a value e_a over the central fifth of the wall height, as indicated in Fig. 4.2. The additional eccentricity is given by an empirical relationship:

$$e_a = t\left(\frac{1}{2400} \; (h_{ef}/t)^2 - 0.015\right) \tag{4.2}$$

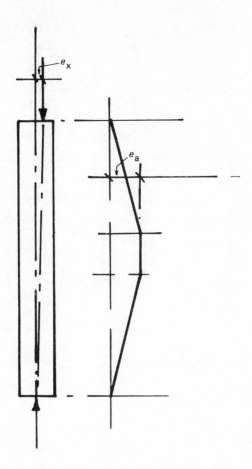

Fig. 4.2 – Assumed eccentricities in BS 5628 formula for design vertical load capacity.

The total eccentricity is then:

$$e_t = 0.6\, e_x + e_a \qquad (4.3)$$

It is possible for e_t to be smaller than e_x, in which case the latter value should be taken as the design eccentricity.

It is next assumed that the load on the wall is resisted by a rectangular stress block with a constant stress of $1.1 f_k / \gamma_m$ (the origin of the coefficient 1.1 is not explained in the code).

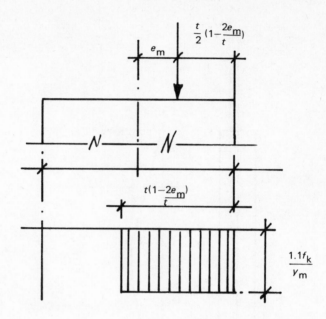

Fig. 4.3 – Assumed stress block in BS 5628 formula for design vertical load capacity.

The width of the stress block, as shown in Fig. 4.3, is

$$t\left(1 - \frac{2e_m}{t}\right) \tag{4.4}$$

and the vertical load capacity of the wall is

$$1.1\left(1 - \frac{2e_m}{t}\right)t \cdot \frac{f_k}{\gamma_m} \tag{4.5}$$

or

$$\beta \cdot t \cdot \frac{f_k}{\gamma_m} \tag{4.6}$$

It will be noted that e_m is the larger of e_x and e_t and is to be not less than $0.05t$. If the eccentricity is less than $0.05t$, β is taken as 1.0. The resulting capacity reduction factors are shown in Fig. 4.4.

As will be apparent, this method of calculating the capacity reduction factor for slenderness and eccentricity embodies a good number of assumptions, and the simple rules given for estimating the eccentricity at the top of a wall are known to be inaccurate – generally the eccentricities calculated by the code method are very much smaller than experimental values. This, however, may be compensated by the empirical formula used for calculating the additional eccentricity, e_a, and by the other assumptions made in calculating the reduction factor. The final result for loadbearing capacity will be of variable accuracy but, protected as it is by a large safety factor, will result in structures of very adequate strength.

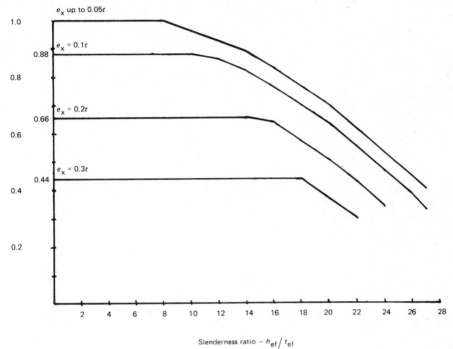

Fig. 4.4 – Capacity reduction factor β in BS 5628.

The remaining part of Section 4 deals with concentrated loads and with walls subjected to lateral loading. Concentrated loads on brickwork are associated with beam bearings, and higher stresses are permitted in the vicinity of these loads. The Code distinguishes three types of beam bearing, as shown in Fig. 4.5. The local design strength, calculated on a uniform bearing stress, for type 1 bearings is $1.25\ f_k/\gamma_m$ and for type 2 bearings $1.5\ f_k/\gamma_m$. Careful inspection of the diagram shown in Fig. 4.5 is necessary to see within which category a particular detail may come, and the logic of the categories is by no means clear. However, it can be seen that under type 1, a slab spanning at right angles to a wall is allowed a 25% increase in design strength, provided that the bearing width is between 50 mm and half the thickness of the wall. Type 2 includes short beam or slab bearings spanning at right angles to the wall, provided that they are more than the bearing width from the end of the wall. Slabs whose bearing length is between six and eight times their bearing width are included in category

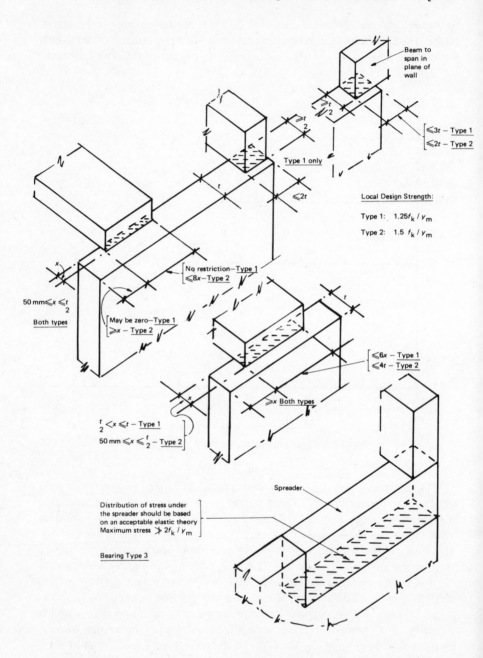

Fig. 4.5 – Design stresses in vicinity of various beam and slab bearings according to BS 5628.

2 and are thus allowed a 50% increase in design strength. A slab resting on the full thickness and width of a wall attracts a 25% increase in design stress provided that it is no longer than six times the wall thickness.

Type 3 bearings envisage the use of a spreader or pad-stone and are permitted a 100% increase in design strength under the spreader. The stress distribution at this location is to be calculated by an acceptable elastic theory.

The basis of these rather complicated provisions is unknown, and there are very few test results for the strength of brickwork under concentrated loading. However, as the previous British Code of Practice, CP 111. allowed a general 50% increase in stresses in the vicinity of concentrated loads without known difficulties, there is little doubt that the provisions of BS 5628 in this respect will be very adequate.

The section on laterally loaded walls was based on a programme of experimental research carried out at the laboratories of the British Ceramic Research Association. For non-loadbearing panels the method is to calculate the design moment given by the formula:

$$\alpha . W_k . \gamma_f . L^2 \tag{4.7}$$

where α =   a bending moment coefficient

γ_f =   partial safety factor for loads

L =   length of the panel between supports

W_k =   characteristic wind load/unit area   .

Values of α for a variety of boundary conditions are given in the Code. They are numerically the same as obtained by yield line formulae for corresponding boundary conditions.

This moment is compared with the design moment of resistance about an axis perpendicular to the plane of the bed joint, equal

to $$\frac{f_{kx} . Z}{\gamma_m}$$

where f_{kx} =   the characteristic strength in flexure

γ_m =   partial safety factor for materials

Z =   section modulus

Obviously everything depends on the successful achievement of f_{kx} on site, and considerable attention must be given to ensuring satisfactory adhesion between bricks and mortar. The best advice that can be given in this respect is to ensure that the bricks are neither kiln-dry nor saturated. Mortar should have as high a water content and retentivity as is consistent with workability. Calcium silicate bricks seem to require particular care in this respect.

Further information is given in this section relating to the lateral resistance of walls with precompression, freestanding walls and retaining walls.

4.2.4 Section 5 : Accidental Damage

The final section of the Code deals with the means of meeting statutory obligations in respect of accidental damage. Special measures are called for only in buildings of over four storeys, although it is necessary to ensure that all buildings are sufficiently robust, as discussed in Chapter 1.

For buildings of five storeys and over, three possible approaches are suggested:

(1) To consider the removal of one horizontal or vertical member at a time, unless it is capable of withstanding a pressure of 34 kN/m^2 in any direction, in which case it may be classed as a 'protected' member.

(2) To provide horizontal ties capable of resisting a specified force and then to consider the effect of removing one vertical member at a time (unless 'protected').

In both of the above cases the building should remain stable, assuming reduced partial safety factors for loads and materials.

(3) To provide horizontal and vertical ties to resist specified forces.

It would appear most practical to adopt the second of the above methods. The first raises the problem of how a floor could be removed without disrupting the walls as well. In the third option, the effect of vertical ties is largely unknown but in one experiment they were found to promote progressive collapse by pulling out wall panels on floors above and below the site of an explosion. If vertical ties are used it would seem advisable to stagger them from storey to storey so as to avoid this effect.

The treatment of accidental damage is discussed in detail in Chapter 9, and the application of the Code provisions to a typical design is given in Chapter 10.

CHAPTER 5

Design for Compressive Loading

5.1 INTRODUCTION

This chapter deals with the compressive strength of walls and columns which are subjected to vertical loads arising from the self weight of the masonry and the adjacent supported floors. Other in-plane forces, such as lateral loads, which produce compression are dealt with in Chapter 6.

In practice, the design of loadbearing walls and columns reduces to the determination of the value of the characteristic compressive strength of the masonry (f_k) and the thickness of the unit required to support the design loads. Once f_k is calculated suitable types of masonry/mortar combinations can be determined from tables or charts.

As stated in Chapter 1 the basic principle of design can be expressed as

Design Vertical Loading $\leqslant$ Design Vertical Load Resistance

in which the term on the left-hand side is determined from the known applied loading and the term on the right is a function of f_k, the slenderness ratio and the eccentricity of loading.

5.2 WALL AND COLUMN BEHAVIOUR UNDER AXIAL LOAD

If it were possible to apply pure axial loading to walls or columns then the type of failure which would occur would be dependent on the slenderness ratio, i.e. the ratio of the effective height to the effective thickness. For short stocky columns, where the slenderness ratio is low, failure would result from compression of the material, whereas for long thin columns and higher values of slenderness ratio, failure would occur from lateral instability.

A typical failure stress curve is shown in Fig. 5.1.

The actual shape of the failure stress curve is also dependent on the properties of the material, and for brickwork it takes the form of the upper curve shown in Fig. 4.4, taking the vertical axis to represent the failure stress rather than β. The failure stress at zero slenderness ratio is dependent on the strength of masonry units and mortar used in the construction and varies between 7.0 and 24 N/mm^2.

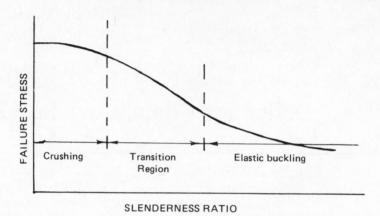

Fig. 5.1 – Failure stress plotted against slenderness ratio.

5.3 WALL AND COLUMN BEHAVIOUR UNDER ECCENTRIC LOAD

It is virtually impossible to apply an axial load to a wall or column since this would require a perfect unit with no fabrication errors. The vertical load will, in general, be eccentric to the central axis and this will produce a bending moment in the member (Fig. 5.2).

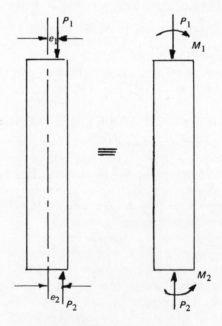

Fig. 5.2 – Eccentric axial loading.

The additional moment can be allowed for in two ways

1) The stresses due to the equivalent axial loads and bending moments can be added using the formula

$$\text{Total stress} = \frac{P}{A} \pm \frac{M}{Z}$$

where A and Z are the area and section modulus of the cross-section, or

2) The interaction between the bending moment and the applied load can be allowed for by reducing the axial load carrying capacity, of the wall or column, by a suitable factor.

The second method is used in BS 5628. The effects of slenderness ratio and eccentricity are combined and appear in the code as the **capacity reduction factor** β. A graph showing the variation of β with slenderness ratio and eccentricity is given in Fig. 4.4.

Note that in BS 5628 the effects of bending moment are neglected for $e < 0.05t$ where t represents the wall or column thickness.

5.4 SLENDERNESS RATIO

This is the ratio of the effective height to the effective thickness, and therefore both of these quantities must be determined for design purposes. The maximum slenderness ratio permitted according to BS 5628 is 27.

5.4.1 Effective Height
The effective height is related to the degree of restraint imposed by the floors and beams which frame into the wall or columns.

Theoretically, if the ends of a strut are free, pinned, or fully fixed then, since the degree of restraint is known, the effective height can be calculated (Fig. 5.3) using the Euler buckling theory.

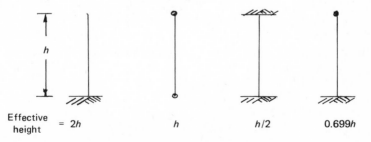

Fig. 5.3 — Effective height for different end conditions.

In practice the end supports to walls and colums do not fit into these neat categories, and engineers have to modify the above values in the light of experience. For example, a wall with concrete floors framing into the top and bottom, from both sides (Fig. 5.4) could be considered as partially fixed at both ends, and for this case the effective length is taken as 0.75h i.e. halfway between the pinned both ends and the fixed both ends cases.

In the above example it is assumed that the degree of fixity is halfway between the pinned and fixed case, but in reality the degree of fixity is dependent on the relative values of the stiffnesses of the floors and walls. For the case of a column with floors framing into both ends the stiffnesses of the floors and columns are of a similar magnitude and the effective height is taken as h, the clear distance between lateral supports (Fig. 5.4).

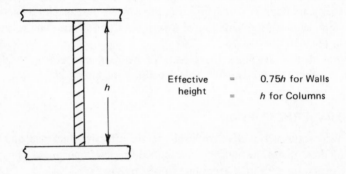

Fig. 5.4 – Effective height for wall/floor and wall/column arrangement.

In BS 5628 the effective height is related to the degree of lateral resistance to movement provided by supports, and the code distinguishes between two types of resistance – simple and enhanced. The term **enhanced resistance** is intended to imply that there is some degree of rotational restraint at the end of the member. Such resistances would arise, for example, if floors span to a wall or column from both sides at the same level or where a concrete floor on one side only has a bearing greater than 90 mm and the building is not more than three storeys.

Conventional values of effective height recommended in BS 5628 are

(i) *Walls*

Enhanced resistance – 0.75h
Simple resistance – h

(ii) *Columns*

With lateral supports in two directions – h

With lateral support in one direction $- h$ (in lateral support direction)

$- 2h$ (in direction in which support is not provided)

(iii) *Columns formed by adjacent openings in walls*

Enhanced resistance $- 0.75h + 0.25$ times height of the taller
of the two openings

Simple resistance $- h$

5.4.2 Effective thickness

The effective thickness of single leaf walls or columns is usually taken as the actual thickness, but for cavity walls or walls with piers other assumptions are made.

Considering the single leaf wall with piers shown in Fig. 5.5(a) it is necessary to decide on the value of the factor K, shown in 5.5(b), which will give a wall of equivalent thickness. Here, the meaning of 'equivalent' is vague since it implies some unknown relationship between the areas and section moduli for the two cases.

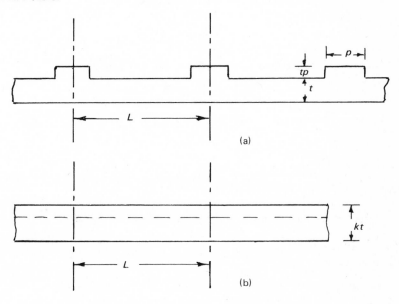

Fig. 5.5 − (a) Single leaf wall with piers; (b) Equivalent wall without piers.

Suggested values for K are given in BS 5628, and these are reproduced below in Table 5.1.

**Table 5.1 K value for effective thickness
of walls stiffened by piers**

L/p	t_p/t		
	1	2	3
6	1.0	1.4	2.0
10	1.0	1.2	1.4
20	1.0	1.0	1.0

The effective thickness for cavity walls, is taken as the greater value of two thirds the sum of the actual thicknesses of the two leaves or the actual thickness of the thicker leaf. For the case of a cavity wall with piers a similar calculation, but introducing the factor K from Table 5.1, is used (Fig. 5.6).

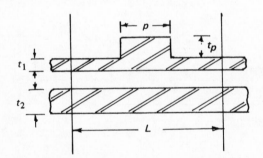

Fig. 5.6 – Cavity wall with piers.

Effective thickness is taken as the greatest value of

(a) $\frac{2}{3}(t_1 + K\,t_2)$ or

(b) t_1 or

(c) $K\,t_2$

According to the code the stiffness coefficients given in Table 5.1 can also be used for a wall stiffened by intersecting walls if the assumption is made that the intersecting walls are equivalent to piers of width equal to the thickness of the intersecting walls and of thickness equal to three times the thickness of the stiffened wall. However, recent experiments do not confirm this.

5.5 CALCULATION OF ECCENTRICITY

In order to determine the value of the eccentricity different simplifying assumptions can be made, and these lead to different methods of calculation. The simplest is the approximate method given in BS 5628, but a more accurate value can be obtained, at the expense of additional calculation, by using a frame analysis.

5.5.1 Approximate Method

(a) The load transmitted by a single floor is assumed to act at one third of the depth of the bearing area from the face of the wall (Fig. 5.7 (a) and (b))

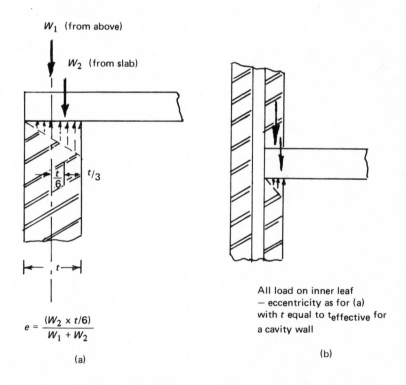

$$e = \frac{(W_2 \times t/6)}{W_1 + W_2}$$

(a)

All load on inner leaf
— eccentricity as for (a)
with t equal to $t_{effective}$ for
a cavity wall

(b)

Fig. 5.7 — (a) Eccentricity for floor/solid wall; (b) Eccentricity for floor/cavity wall.

(b) For a continuous floor, the load from each side is assumed to act at one sixth of the thickness of the appropriate face (Fig. 5.8(a))
(c) Where joist hangers are used the load is assumed to act at the centre of the joist bearing area of the hanger (Fig. 5.8(b)).

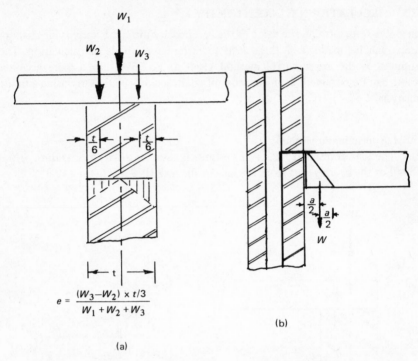

$$e = \frac{(W_3 - W_2) \times t/3}{W_1 + W_2 + W_3}$$

(a)

(b)

Fig. 5.8 – (a) Eccentricity for continuous floor/wall; (b) Assumed load position with joist hanger.

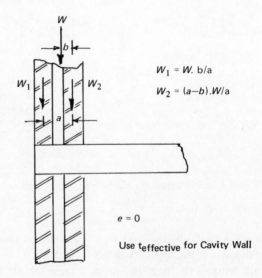

$W_1 = W. \, b/a$

$W_2 = (a-b).W/a$

$e = 0$

Use $t_{\text{effective}}$ for Cavity Wall

Fig. 5.9 – Eccentricity for cavity wall.

(d) If the applied vertical load acts between the centroid of the two leaves of a cavity wall it should be replaced by statically equivalent axial loads in the two leaves (Fig. 5.9).

Note that the total vertical load on a wall above the lateral support being considered is assumed to be axial.

5.5.2 Frame Analysis

If the wall bending moment and axial load are calculated for any joint in a multi-storey framed structure then the eccentricity can be determined by dividing the moment by the axial load.

The required moment and axial load can be determined using a normal rigid frame analysis. This approach is reasonable when the wall compression is high enough to contribute to the rigidity of the joints, but would lead to inaccuracies when the compression is small.

The complete frame analysis can be avoided by a partial analysis which assumes that the far ends of members (floors and walls) attached to the joint under consideration are pinned (Fig. 5.10).

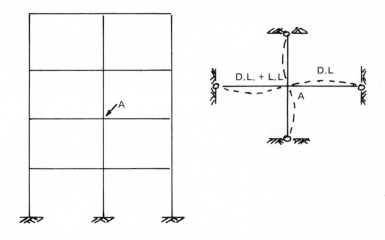

Fig. 5.10 – Multi-storey frame and typical joint.

The wall bending moments for the most unfavourable loading conditions can now be determined using moment–distribution or slope–deflection methods.

More sophisticated methods which allow for the relative rotation of the wall and slab at the joints and changing wall stiffness due to tension cracking in flexure are being developed.

Note: The eccentricity calculated above is the value at the top of the wall or column where the floor frames into the wall. In BS 5628 the eccentricity is assumed to vary from the calculated value at the top of the wall to zero at the bottom of the wall, subject to an additional eccentricity being considered to cover slenderness effects (see Chapter 4, page 62).

5.6 VERTICAL LOAD RESISTANCE

The resistance of walls or columns to vertical loading is obviously related to the characteristic strength of the material used for construction, and it has been shown above that the value of the characteristic strength used must be reduced to allow for the slenderness ratio and the eccentricity of loading. If we require the *design* vertical load resistance, then, the characteristic strength, which is related to the strength at failure, must be further reduced by dividing by a safety factor for the material.

As shown in Chapter 4 the British Code introduces a capacity reduction factor β which allows simultaneously for effects of eccentricity and slenderness ratio. It should be noted that these values of β are for use with the assumed notional values of eccentricity given in the code, and that if the eccentricity is determined by a frame type analysis which takes account of continuity then different capacity reduction factors should be used.

If tensile strains are developed over part of a wall or column then there is a reduction in the effective area of the cross-section since it can be assumed that the area under tension has cracked. This effect is of importance for high values of eccentricity and slenderness ratio, and the Swedish Code allows for it by introducing the ultimate strain value for the determination of the reduction factor.

5.6.1 Design vertical load resistance of walls
Using the principles outlined above the design vertical load resistance per unit length of wall is given by $(\beta t f_k)/\gamma_m$ where γ_m is the partial safety factor for the material and β is obtained from Fig. 4.4,

5.6.2 Design vertical load resistance of columns
For columns the design vertical load resistance is given by $(\beta b t f_k)/\gamma_m$, but for this case the following rules apply to the selection of β from Fig. 4.4.

Eccentricity at top of column about major axis	Eccentricity at top of column about minor axis	Selection of β
$<0.05b$	$<0.05t$	Use upper curve of Fig. 4.4 with t_{ef} appropriate to minor axis

Continued next page

Contined from previous page

Eccentricity at top of column about major axis	Eccentricity at top of column about minor axis	Selection of β
$<0.05b$	$>0.05t$	Use Fig. 4.4 with both eccentricity and slenderness ratio appropriate to minor axis
$>0.05b$	$<0.05t$	Use Fig. 4.4 with eccentricity appropriate to major and slenderness ratio to minor axis

If the eccentricities at the top of column about the major and minor axis are greater than $0.05b$ and $0.05t$ respectively then the code recommends that the values of β can be determined from the equations given in Appendix B. The method can be summarised as follows,

About XX axis
1) The design eccentricity e_m about XX is defined as the larger value of e_x and e_t

where $e_t = 0.6e_x + t \left[\dfrac{1}{2400} \left(\dfrac{h_{ef}}{t} \right)^2 - 0.015 \right]$

and $(h\,ef/t)$ is the slenderness ratio about the minor axis.

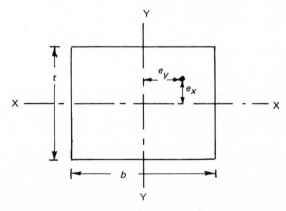

Fig. 5.11 – Column cross-section.

2) The value of β is calculated from

$$\beta = 1.1\ (1 - 2\,e_m/t)$$

About YY axis
Use a similar procedure using e_y and the slenderness ratio about the major axis but note that no slenderness effect need be considered when the slenderness ratio is less than 6, (see example below).

Example
Determine the values of β for a solid brickwork column of cross-section 215 mm $\times$ 430 mm and effective height about both axes of 2500 mm if the eccentricity at the top of the columns about the major and minor axes are

a) 25 mm and 10 mm and

b) 60 mm and 20 mm respectively.

Solution (a)

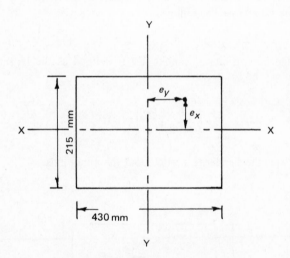

Fig. 5.12 — Dimensions of worked example.

$$e_x = 10 = 0.046t \ \text{i.e.} \ <0.05t$$

$$e_y = 25 = 0.058b \ \text{i.e.} \ >0.05b$$

Therefore use Fig. 4.4 with eccentricity appropriate to major axis YY (25 mm) and slenderness ratio appropriate to minor axis. S. R. = 2500/215 = 11.63. Using Fig. 4.4, $\beta \simeq 0.93$

(b) $e_x = 20 = 0.093t$ i.e. $>0.05t$

  $e_y = 60 = 0.139b$ i.e. $>0.05b$

About XX axis

  $e_m = e_x = 20$ mm

or $e_m = e_t = 0.6 \times 20 + 215$ $[(1/2400)(2500/215)^2 - 0.015]$

      $= 12 + 8.89 = 20.89$ mm

  $\beta_{xx} = 1.1 (1 - (2 \times 20.89/215)) = 0.89.$

About YY axis

  $e_m = e_y = 60$ mm

or $e_m = e_t = 0.6 \times 60 + 430$ $[(1/2400) \times (2500/430)^2 - 0.015]$

      $= 36 + 430 [0.014 - 0.015].$

The bracketed term is negative because the slenderness ratio is less than 6 and therefore for this case no additional term due to slenderness effect is required. That is $e_m = 60$ mm and $\beta_{yy} = 1.1 (1 - (2 \times 60/430)) = 0.79.$

Note: The design vertical load resistance for the above example would be

  a) $\dfrac{\beta b t f_k}{\gamma_m} = \dfrac{0.93 \times 215 \times 430 \times f_k}{\gamma_m}$

and b) $\dfrac{\beta b t f_k}{\gamma_m} = \dfrac{0.89 \times 215 \times 430 \times f_k}{\gamma_m}.$

That is, the largest value of β_{xx} and β_{yy} is used in order to ensure that the smaller value of f_k will be determined when the design vertical load resistance is equated to the design vertical load.

5.6.3 Design Vertical Load resistance of cavity walls or columns

The design vertical load resistance for cavity walls or columns can be determined using the methods outlined in sections 5.6.1 and 5.6.2 if the vertical loading is first replaced by the statically equivalent axial load on each leaf. The effective thickness of the cavity wall or column is used for determining the slenderness ratio for each leaf of the cavity.

5.6.4 Design vertical strength for concentrated loads (See Fig. 4.5)

Increased stresses occur beneath concentrated loads from beams and lintels, etc., and the combined effect of these local stresses with the stresses due to other loads should be checked. The concentrated load is assumed to be uniformly distributed over the bearing area, and in BS 5628 two design checks are suggested,

a) at the bearing assuming a local design bearing strength of either $1.25\,f_k/\gamma_m$ or $1.5\,f_k/\gamma_m$ depending on the type of bearing.

b) at a distance of $0.4h$ below the bearing where the design strength is assumed to be $\beta f_k/\gamma_m$.

The concentrated load is assumed to be dispersed within a zone contained by lines extending downwards at 45° from the edges of the loaded area. (Fig. 5.13).

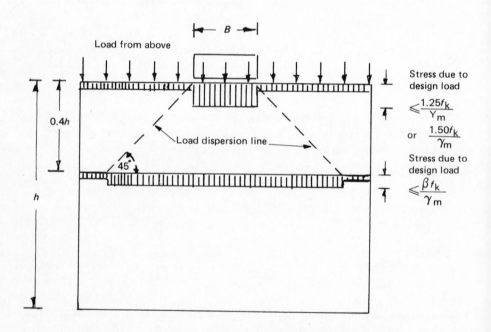

Fig. 5.13 – Stress distribution due to concentrated load (BS 5628).

The code also makes reference to the special case of a spreader beam located at the end of a wall and spanning in its plane. For this case the maximum stress at the bearing, combined with stressses due to other loads, should not exceed $2.0f_k/\gamma_m$ although the code states that the actual stress distribution under the spreader may be derived from an acceptable elastic theory.

5.7 VERTICAL LOADING

Details about characteristic dead and imposed loads and partial safety factors have been given in Chapter 4, and values of the design vertical loads will already have been determined for the calculation of the eccentricities. The design process for vertical loading is completed by equating the design vertical loading to the appropriate design vertical load resistance and using the resulting equation to determine the value of the characteristic compressive strength of the masonry f_k. Typically the equation takes the form

$$\Sigma W. \, KN/m = \beta t f_k / \gamma_m \qquad\qquad (5.1)$$

Generally the calculation of ΣW involves the summation of products of the partial safety factor for load (γ_f) with the appropriate characteristic load (G_k and Q_k). This is discussed in Chapter 4 and illustrated in Chapter 10.

Using standard tables or charts (Fig. 4.1) and modification factors where applicable, the compressive strength of the brick/block units and the required mortar strength to provide the necessary value of f_k can be obtained.

Examples of the calculation for an inner solid brick wall and an external cavity wall are given in the next section.

5.8 MODIFICATION FACTORS

The value of f_k used in Fig. 4.1, in order to determine a suitable brick/mortar combination, is sometimes modified to allow for the effects of small plan area or narrow brick walls.

5.8.1 Small plan area
If the horizontal cross-sectional area (A) is less than 0.2 m^2 then the value of f_k determined from an equation similar to (5.1) is divided† by a factor $(0.70 + 1.5A)$.

5.8.2 Narrow brick walls
If the thickness of the wall is equal to the width of the brick then the values of f_k determined from an equation similar to (5.1) is divided† by 1.15.

---

† Some designers include the modification factors in the basic equation (5.1) where they appear as a multiplication factor on the right-hand side, e.g. for narrow walls, equation (5.1) could be rewritten $\Sigma W = \beta t (1.15 f_k)/\gamma$.

5.9 EXAMPLES

Example 1   Internal Brick Wall

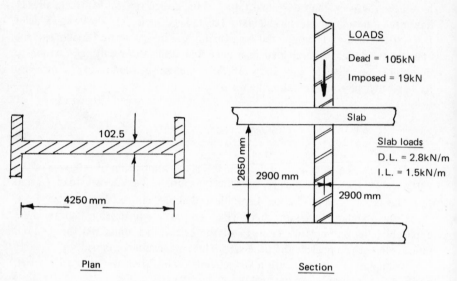

Fig. 5.14 — Plan and section details for example 1.

(1) *Loading* (per metre run of wall)

	Dead load (kN/m)	Imposed load (kN/m)
Load from above	105.0	19.0
Self weight of wall	17.0	—
Load from left slab	4.1	2.2
Load from right slab	4.1	2.2

(2) *Safety Factors*

     For material strength (γ_m) = 3.5

     For loading (γ_f) Dead load = 1.4

         Imposed load = 1.6

(3) *Design Vertical Loading* (Fig. 5.15)

     Load from above (W_1) = 1.4 × 105 + 1.6 × 19 = 177.4 kN/m

     Load from left (W_2)

         Dead Load only = 1.4 × 4.1 = 5.7 kN/m

         Imposed Load = 5.7 + 1.6 × 2.2 = 9.2 kN/m

Load from right (W_3)

Dead Load only	= 5.7 kN/m
Dead + Imposed	= 9.2 kN/m
Wall self weight = 1.4 × 17	= 23.8 kN/m

(4) *Eccentricity*

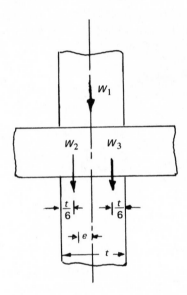

Fig. 5.15 – Loading arrangement for eccentricity calculation.

See section 5.5.1 (b)

(a) With full D.L. + I.L. on each slab there will be no eccentricity since $W_2 = W_3$.

(b) With only one slab loaded with superimposed load; that is: $W_2 = 9.2$, $W_3 = 5.7$.

Taking moments about centre line

$$\Sigma We = W_2 \times (t/3) - W_3 \times (t/3)$$

$$e = \frac{(9.2 - 5.7) \times (t/3)}{9.2 + 5.7 + 177.4 + (1.4 \times 17)} = 0.005t;$$

that is, e is $<0.05t$ and can be neglected. The small value of e results from the high precompression.

(5) *Slenderness Ratio*

Effective height = 0.75 × 2650 = 1988 mm

Effective thickness = Actual thickness = 102.5 mm

Slenderness ratio = 1988/102.5 = 19.4.

(6) *Design Vertical Load Resistance*

Using the slenderness ratio of 19.4 and the eccentricity of $<0.05t$ the capacity reduction factor β can be interpolated from Fig. 4.4, $\beta = 0.72$.
Assuming t in mm and f_k in N/mm^2,

$$\text{Design vertical load resistance} = \frac{\beta t f_k}{\gamma_m} \ N/mm$$

$$= \frac{0.72 \times 102.5 \times f_k}{3.5} \ N/mm$$

$$= 21.09 \ f_k \ N/mm \ (\text{or } kN/m)$$

(7) *Determination of f_k*

Design vertical load = Design vertical load resistance
$(177.4 + 9.2 + 9.2 + 23.8) \ kN/m = 21.09 \ f_k \ kN/m$

$$f_k = 10.41 \ N/mm^2$$

(8) *Modification factors for f_k*

(a) Horizontal cross-sectional area of wall = 0.1025 × 4.25 = 0.44 m^2

Since $A > 0.2 \ m^2$, no modification factor for area.

(b) Narrow brickwall.

Since wall is one brick thick, modification factor = 1.15.

(9) *Required value of f_k*

$$f_k = 10.41/1.15 = 9.05 \ N/mm^2.$$

(10) *Selection of brick-mortar combination*

Using Fig. 4.1 to select a suitable brick/mortar combination. Any of the following would provide the required value of f_k.

Mortar Designation	Compressive strength of bricks (N/mm²)
(iii)	38.9
(ii)	33.3
(i)	26.9

Example 2   External Cavity Wall

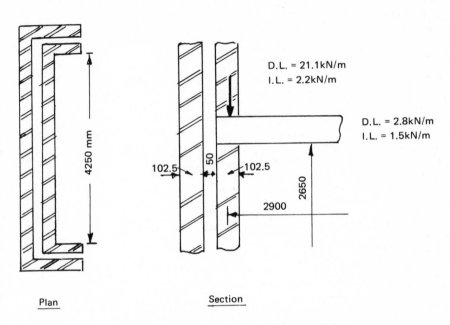

Fig. 5.16 – Plan and section details for example 2.

(1) *Loads on inner leaf*

	D.L.(kN/m)	I.L.(kN/m)
Load from above	21.1	2.2
Self weight of wall	17.0	—
Load from slab	4.1	2.2

(2) *Safety Factors*

$$\gamma_m = 3.5$$
$$\gamma_f(\text{D. L.}) = 1.4$$
$$\gamma_f(\text{L.L.}) = 1.6$$

(3) *Design Vertical Loading* (Fig. 5.17)

$W_1 = 1.4 \times 21.1 + 1.6 \times 22.2 = 33.1$ kN/m

$W_2 = 1.4 \times 4.1 + 1.6 \times 22.2 = 9.2$ kN/m

W_s = Self weight of wall = $1.4 \times 17 = 23.8$ kN/m

Total vertical design load = 66.1 kN/m

(4) *Eccentricity*

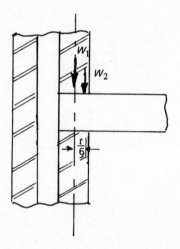

Fig. 5.17 – Loading arrangement for eccentricity calculations.

See section 5.5.1. Taking moments about centre line

$$(W_1 + W_2 + W_s)e = W_2 t/6$$

$$e = \frac{9.2 \times 102.5}{6(33.1 + 9.2 + 23.8)} = 2.38 \text{ mm},$$

that is, $e < 0.05t$ and eccentricity can be neglected.

It can be shown that the ratio $(W_1 + W_s)/W_2$ must be less that 2.33 in order that the eccentricity is greater than $0.05t$.

(5) *Slenderness Ratio*

Effective height = $0.75 \times 2650 = 1988$ mm

Effective thickness = $\frac{2}{3}(102.5 + 102.5) = 136$ mm

Slenderness ratio = 1988/136 = 14.6

(6) *Design Vertical Load Resistance*

Using the slenderness ratio of 14.6 and eccentricity $<0.05t$ the capacity reduction factor β from Fig. 4.4 is $\beta = 0.87$. Assuming t in mm and f_k in N/mm^2.

Design vertical load resistance $= \beta t f_k / \gamma_m = 0.87 \times 102.5 \times f_k / 3.5$
$= 25.48 f_k$ (N/mm or kN/m)

(7) *Determination of f_k*

Design vertical load $=$ Design vertical load resistance

$(33.1 + 9.2 + 23.8)$ kN/m $= 25.48 f_k$ kN/m

$f_k = 2.59$ N/mm^2

(8) *Modification factors for f_k*

(a) Horizontal cross-sectional area $-$ $4.25 \times 0.1025 = 0.44$ m^2

Greater than 0.2 m^2 $\therefore$ no modification factor for area.

(b) Narrow brick wall

Wall is one brick thick; modifications factor $= 1.15$

(9) *Required Value of f_k*

$f_k = 2.59/1.15 = 2.25$ N/mm^2.

(10) *Selection of brick mortar combination*

Use Fig. 4.1 to select a suitable brick/mortar combination – nominal in this case.

CHAPTER 6

Design for Wind Loading

6.1 INTRODUCTION

Conventionally, in wind loading analysis, wind pressure is assumed to act statically on a structure. Such forces depend at a particular site on the mean hourly wind speed, the estimation of an appropriate gust factor, shape and pressure coefficients and the effect of local topography. The wind force calculated from these factors is assumed to act as an equivalent uniformly distributed load on the building for its full height. Sometimes the wind velocity or the gust factor is assumed variable with the height of the building, so that the intensity of the equivalent uniformly distributed load varies accordingly. In the United Kingdom, wind loads on buildings are calculated from the provisions of the Code of Practice CP 3 Chapter V Part 2, 1970.

Whilst brickwork is strong in compression, it is very weak in tension, thus engineering design for wind loading may be needed, not only for multi-storey structures, but also for some single-storey structures. Fig. 6.1 shows how a typical brick building resists lateral forces. It can be seen that two problems in wind loading design need to be considered: 1) overall stability of the building and 2) the strength of individual wall panels. In this chapter overall stability of the building will be considered.

6.2 OVERALL STABILITY

To provide stability or to stop 'card-house' type of collapse, shear walls are provided parallel to the direction of lateral loading. This is similar to diagonal bracing in a steel frame building. In brickwork structures, adequate length of walls must be provided in two directions to resist wind loads. In addition, floors must be stiff and strong enough to transfer the loads to the walls by diaphragm action. The successful action of a horizontal diaphragm requires that it would be well tied into the supporting shear walls. Chapter 1, section 1.2, explains in detail how lateral stability is provided in various types of brick buildings, through suitable wall arrangements.

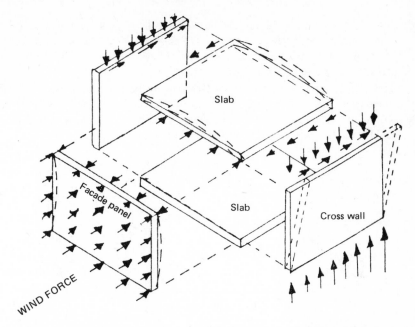

Fig. 6.1 – Showing the action of wind forces on a building. Wind force is resisted by the facade panel owing to bending, and transferred via floor slabs to the cross or shear wall and finally to the ground. (Structural Clay Products Ltd.)

6.3 THEORETICAL METHODS FOR WIND LOAD ANALYSIS

The calculation of the lateral stiffness and stresses in a system of symmetrically placed shear walls without openings subjected to wind loading is straight forward and involves simple bending theory only. Fig. 6.2 gives an illustration of such a system of shear walls.

Because of bending and shear the walls deform as cantilevers, and since the horizontal diaphragm is rigid the deflections at slab level must be the same. The deflection of individual walls is

given by:

$$\triangle_1 = \frac{W_1 h^3}{3EI_1} + \frac{\lambda W_1 h}{AG} \tag{6.1}$$

$$\triangle_2 = \frac{W_2 h^3}{3EI_2} + \frac{\lambda W_2 h}{AG} \tag{6.2}$$

$$\triangle_1 = \triangle_2 \tag{6.3}$$

$$2W_1 + W_2 = W \tag{6.4}$$

where W_1, W_2 = lateral force acting on individual wall, $\triangle_1$, $\triangle_2$ = deflection of walls A = area of walls, h = height, E = modulus of elasticity, G = modulus of rigidity, I_1, I_2 = second moment of area, λ = shear deformation coefficient (1.2 for rectangular section, 1.0 flanged section).

The proportion of the lateral load carried by each wall can be obtained from equations 6.1 to 6.4. The first term in equations 6.1 and 6.2 is bending deflection and second is that due to shear. The shear deflection is normally neglected if the height:width ratio is greater than 5.

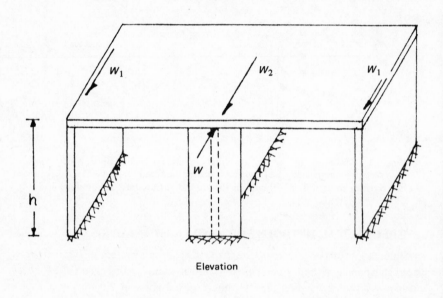

Elevation

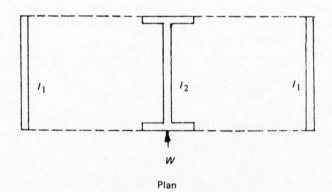

Plan

Fig. 6.2 – A system of shear walls resisting wind force.

6.3.1 Coupled shear walls

Shear walls with openings present a much more complex problem. Openings normally occur in vertical rows throughout the height of the wall, and the connection between the wall sections is provided either by beams forming the part of the wall or by floor slabs or by a combination of both. Such walls are described as 'coupled shear walls', 'pierced shear walls or 'shear walls with openings. Fig. 6.3 (a) shows a simple five-storey high coupled shear wall structure.

There are five basic methods of analysis for the estimation of wind stresses and deflection in such shear walls; namely: i) cantilever approach, ii) equivalent frame, iii) wide column frame, iv) continuum, and v) finite element.

Fig. 6.3(b) to (f) shows the idealisation of shear walls with openings for each of these methods.

6.3.2 Cantilever Approach

The structure is assumed to consist of a series of vertical cantilever walls which are made to deflect together at each level by the floor slabs. That is, the slabs transmit direct forces only, bending being neglected. The wind moment is divided amongst the walls in proportion to their flexural rigidities. This is the most commonly used method for the design of brickwork structures. The deflection of the wall is given by:

$$\Delta = \frac{w_1}{EI_1} \left[\frac{x^4}{24} - \frac{h^3 x}{6} + h^4/_8 \right] \tag{6.5}$$

Also

$$\Delta = \frac{w_2}{EI_2} \left[x^4/_{24} - \frac{h^3 x}{6} + h^4/_8 \right] \tag{6.6}$$

where

$$w_1 = \frac{w}{I_1 + I_2} \cdot I_1 \text{ and } w_2 = \frac{w}{I_1 + I_2} \cdot I_2$$

w — total uniformly distributed wind load/unit height, h — height of building
x — distance of section under consideration from the top.
I_1 and I_2 — second moment of areas (Fig. 6.3(b)).

6.3.3 Equivalent Frame

In this method, the walls and slabs are replaced by columns and beams having the same flexural rigidities as the walls and floor slabs respectively. The span of the beams is taken to be the distance between the centroidal axes of adjacent columns (Fig. 6.3(c)). The axial and shear deformations of beams and columns may be neglected or may be included if the structure is analysed by using any standard computer program which takes these deformations into account.

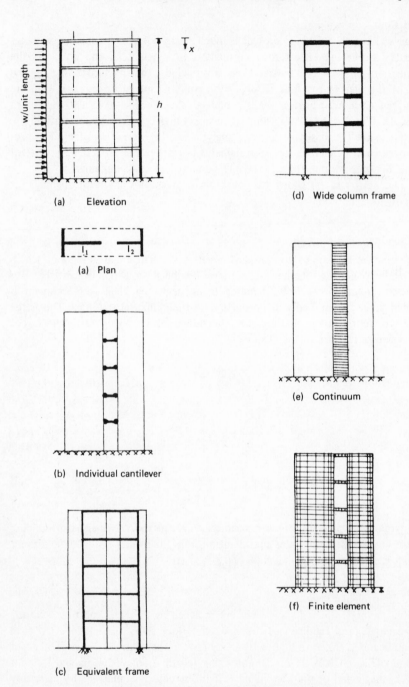

(a)   Elevation

(a)   Plan

(b)   Individual cantilever

(c)   Equivalent frame

(d)   Wide column frame

(e)   Continuum

(f)   Finite element

Fig. 6.3 – Idealisation of shear walls with opening for theoretical analysis.

6.3.4 Wide Column Frame

The wide column frame is a further refinement of the equivalent frame method. The structure is idealised as in the equivalent frame method except that the interconnecting members are assumed to be of infinite rigidity for part of their length; i.e. from the centroidal axes of the columns to the opening as in Fig. 6.3(d). The system can be analysed by using a standard computer program or by conventional analysis which may or may not take into consideration the axial and shear deformation of the beams and columns.

6.3.5 Continuum

In this method, the discrete system of connecting slabs or beams is replaced by an equivalent shear medium (Fig. 6.3(e)) which is assumed continuous over the full height of the walls, and a point of contra-flexure is taken at the centre of the medium. Axial deformation of the medium and shear deformations of the walls are neglected.

Basically, the various continuum theories put forward for the analysis of a coupled shear wall, are the same except for the choice of the redundant function. Readers interested are advised to consult the specialised literature† for the derivation of the theory.

6.3.6 Finite Element Analysis

In finite element analysis the structure is divided into a finite number of small triangular or rectangular elements, (Fig. 6.3(f)) which are assumed to be connected only at their nodes. Application of the equations of equilibrium of the forces acting at these nodal points leads to a number of simultaneous equations which can be solved with the aid of a computer. The method provides a very powerful analytical tool, and suitable computer programs are readily available which can deal with any type of complex structure. However, this may prove to be a costly exercise in practical design situations.

6.3.7 Selection of Analytical Method

Although these methods are used in practice for analysis and design of rows of plane walls connected by slabs or beams, the analysis of a complex three-dimensional multi-storey structure presents an even more difficult problem. Furthermore, it has been observed experimentally that the results of these methods of analysis are not necessarily consistent with the behaviour of actual brick shear wall structure even in a simple two-dimensional cases. The difference between the experimental and theoretical results may be due to the assumptions regarding interactions between the elements, which in a practical structure may not be valid because of the method of construction and the jointing materials.

---

† *Tall Buildings – The Proceedings of a Symposium on Tall Buildings,* edited by A. Coull and B. Stafford Smith, Pergamon Press, 1967.

Fig. 6.4 – Test structure.   PLAN

Three Jacks per Floor

6.25 m

To investigate the behaviour of a three-dimensional brickwork structure and the validity of the various analytical methods, a full-scale test building was built (Fig. 6.4) in a disused quarry, and lateral loads were applied by jacking at each floor level against the quarry face, which had been previously lined with concrete to give an even working face. The deflections and strains were recorded at various loads. The three-dimensional structure was replaced by an equivalent two-dimensional wall and beam system having the same areas and moments of inertia as the actual structure and analysed by the various methods described in this chapter. The theoretical and experimental deflections are compared in Fig. 6.5.

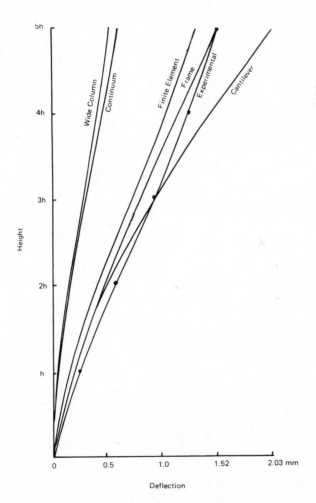

Fig. 6.5 − Comparison of experimental and theoretical deflction results for an equivalent uniform load of 894 N/m² over the loaded face of the building.

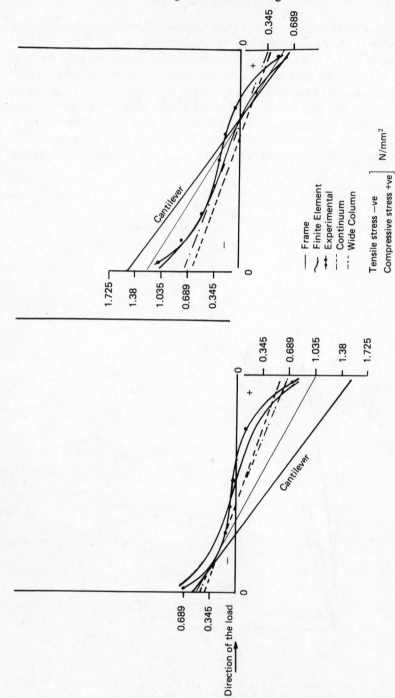

Fig. 6.6 – Stress distribution across the shear walls at the base for an equivalent uniform load of 894 N/m² over the loaded face of the building (only one-half of the structure is shown).

The strain and thus stress distribution across the shear wall near ground level was nonlinear, as shown in Fig. 6.6. Most theoretical methods, with the exception of finite elements, assume a linear variation of stress across the shear wall and thus did not give accurate results. The comparisons between the various analytical methods considered (namely, simple cantilever, frame, wide column frame, and shear continuum method) with experimental results strongly suggest that the best approximation to the actual behaviour of a brickwork structure of this type is obtained by replacing the actual structure by an equivalent rigid frame in which the columns have the same sectional properties as the walls with interconnecting slabs spanning between the axes of the columns. The continuum or wide column frame methods do not seem to give satisfactory results for brickwork structures, hence their use is not advisable. Finite element analysis may be justified only in special cases, and will give the nonlinear stress distribution, which cannot be reproduced by other methods.

The cantilever method of analysis is an oversimplification of the behaviour and is very conservative. For this reason, and because it is simple to carry out, it may be used for preliminary estimates of the bending moments and shearing forces in the walls of a building arising from wind loads. It should be noted, however, that this procedure neglects bending of the interconnecting beams or slabs, and this may require consideration.

6.4 LOAD DISTRIBUTION BETWEEN UNSYMMETRICALLY ARRANGED SHEAR WALLS

When a system of shear walls of uniform cross-section throughout their height is not symmetrical either through uneven spacing of walls or non-uniform distribution of mass, the resultant of the wind loads will not pass through the shear centre, i.e. the centroid of the moments of inertia, and a twisting moment will be applied to the building as illustrated in Fig. 6.7 (a). Similarly, torsion will be induced in a symmetrical building, if the resultant of the applied forces do not pass through the shear centre.

The load W on the structure can be replaced by a load acting at the shear centre as in a symmetrical case, together with a twisting moment equal to $W.e$ as in Fig. 6.7 (b) or (c). In the case of symmetry, the load is distributed to each wall in proportion to their stiffness, since the deflection of walls must be the same at floor level, hence

$$W_A = \frac{WI_A}{I_A + I_B + I_C} = \frac{WI_A}{\Sigma I} \tag{6.7}$$

$$W_B = \frac{WI_B}{\Sigma I} \ , \ W_C = \frac{WI_C}{\Sigma I} \tag{6.8}$$

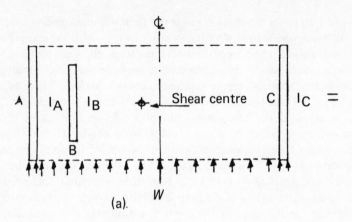

(a).

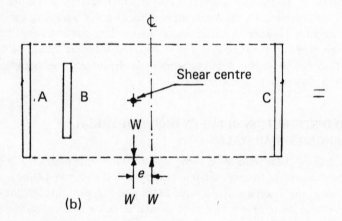

(b)

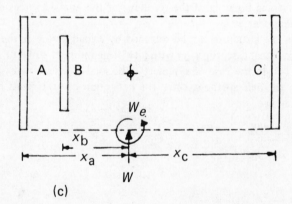

(c)

Fig. 6.7 – Unsymmetrical shear walls, subjected to wind loading.

Due to twisting moment $(W.e)$, the walls are subjected to further loading of magnitude W_A', W_B' and W_C' respectively. The loading in walls A and B will be *negative* and in wall C will be *positive*.

Assume the deflection of walls due to twisting moment is equal to $\triangle_a$, $\triangle_b$ and $\triangle_c$ as shown in the Fig. 6.8.

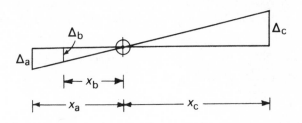

As the floor is rigid, $\quad \triangle_b = \triangle_a/x_a \cdot x_b$ $\qquad\qquad$ (6.9)

$$\triangle_c = \triangle_a/x_a \cdot x_c \qquad\qquad (6.10)$$

Also $\quad \triangle_a = W_A'h^3/KEI_A \qquad\qquad$ (6.11)

where K is deflection constant

$$\triangle_b = W_B'h^3/KEI_B \qquad\qquad (6.12)$$

Substituting the value of $\triangle_b$ from (6.9) and $\triangle_a$ from (6.11), we get

$$(\triangle_a/x_a) \cdot x_b = W_B'h^3/KEI_B \qquad\qquad (6.13)$$

or $\qquad (x_b/x_a)(W_A'/I_A) = W_B'/I_B$

or $\qquad W_B' = (W_A'I_B/I_A) \cdot (x_b/x_a) \qquad\qquad$ (6.13)

similarly, $\qquad W_C' = (W_A'I_c/I_A) \cdot (x_c/x_a) \qquad\qquad$ (6.14)

Now the sum of the moments of all the forces about the shear centre of all the walls must be equal to the twisting moment, hence

$$W_A'x_a + W_B'x_b + W_C'x_c = W.e \qquad\qquad (6.15)$$

or $\qquad W_A'[x_a + (I_B/I_A) \cdot (x_b^2/x_a) + (I_C/I_A) \cdot (x_c^2/x_a)] = W.e$

or $\qquad W_A{}' = \dfrac{W.e \,.\, I_A \,.\, x_a}{I_A x_a{}^2 + I_B x_b{}^2 + I_c x_c{}^2} = \dfrac{W.e.x_a \,.\, I_a}{\Sigma Ix^2} \quad,$ $\qquad\qquad$ (6.15)

similarly, $\quad W_B{}' = W.e.x_b/\Sigma Ix^2 \;$ and $\; W_c{}' = W.e.x_c \,.\, I_c/\Sigma Ix^2 \quad.$

The load in each wall will be the algebraic sum of loads calculated from equations 6.7, 6.8 and 6.15. In other words, the load resisted by each wall can be expressed as,

$$W_n = \frac{WI_n}{\Sigma I} \pm \frac{W.e.x_n I_n}{\Sigma Ix^2} \qquad\qquad (6.16)$$

The second term in the equation is positive for walls on the same side of the centroid as the load W.

CHAPTER 7

Lateral Load Analysis
of Brickwork Panels

7.1 GENERAL

In any typical loadbearing masonry structure two types of wall panel resist lateral pressure, which could arise from wind forces or the effect of explosion. These panels can be classified as follows:

i) Panels with precompression, i.e. panels subjected to both vertical and lateral loading.

ii) Panels without precompression, i.e. panels subjected to self-weight and lateral loading.

7.2 ANALYSIS OF PANELS WITH PRECOMPRESSION

The lateral strength of panels with precompression depends on the following factors:

i) Flexural tensile strength

ii) Initial precompression

iii) Stiffness of the building against upward thrust

iv) Boundary conditions.

7.2.1 Flexural tensile strength
The flexural tensile strength of brickwork normal to the bed joint is very low, therefore it may be ignored in the lateral load design of panels with precompression without loss of great accuracy.

7.2.2 Initial Precompression
As will be shown in Section 7.3, the lateral strength of a wall depends on the vertical precompression applied to it. Normally this is taken to be the dead load of the structure supported by it, but if settlement occurs, it is possible

for a proportion of this load to be redistributed to other parts of the structure. This explained in simplified terms in Fig. 7.1. Relative settlement of the right-hand wall shown in the diagram will induce bending moments in the floor slabs which, in turn, will reduce the loading on this wall. The quantitative significance of this effect is shown in Fig. 7.2 which is based on measurements taken on an actual structure. As may be seen from this, relative settlement of only one or two millimetres can reduce the precompression by a large percentage.

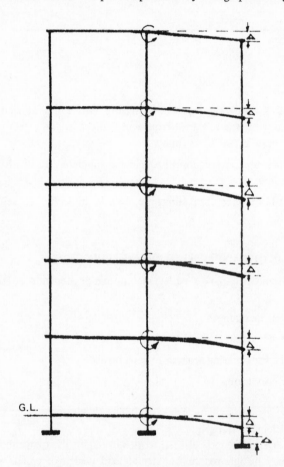

Fig. 7.1 – Redistribution of load due to settlement.

7.2.3 Stiffness of a Building

Just before collapse a wall under lateral loading tends to lift the structure above it by a certain distance, as shown in Fig. 7.3. The uplift depends on the thickness of the wall. This is the opposite effect to that described in relation to settlement and results in an additional precompression on the wall, the value depending on

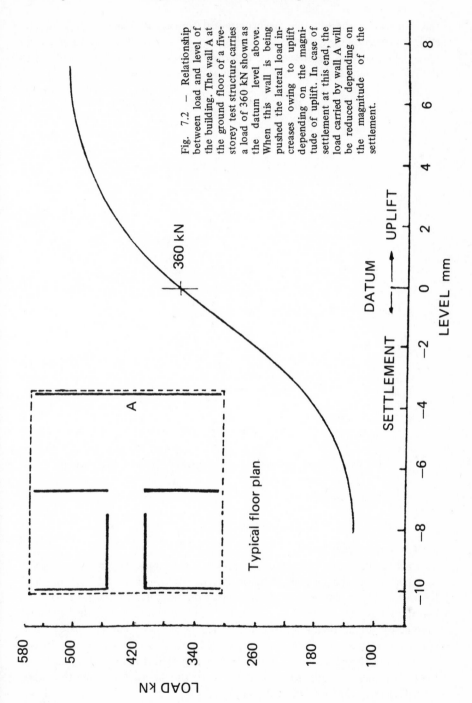

Fig. 7.2 – Relationship between load and level of the building. The wall A at the ground floor of a five-storey test structure carries a load of 360 kN shown as the datum level above. When this wall is being pushed the lateral load increases owing to uplift depending on the magnitude of uplift. In case of settlement at this end, the load carried by wall A will be reduced depending on the magnitude of the settlement.

the stiffness of the building against upward thrust. As shown in Fig. 7.2 the stiffness of a building, however, is highly indeterminate and nonlinear and in practical design this additional precompression may be ignored. This will add to the safety of such walls against failure under lateral pressure.

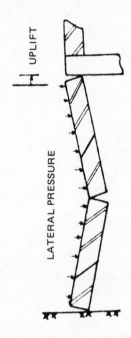

Fig. 7.3 – Showing uplift of the slab at the time of collapse of wall beneath it.

7.2.4 Boundary conditions
In practice, the walls in loadbearing masonry structures may be supported at top and bottom and may, in addition, be supported at the sides by return walls. Returns can give extra strength depending on the ratio of the length to the height of the wall attached to the return, the tensile strength of the brick and the number of headers tying the wall to the return. In a normal English bond alternate courses of headers are used to tie the wall to its return. In the approximate theory described in the next paragraph, it has been assumed that the return does not fail. However, the designer should check whether the return can safely carry the load imposed on it.

7.3 AN APPROXIMATE THEORY FOR THE LATERAL LOAD ANALYSIS OF WALLS SUBJECTED TO PRECOMPRESSION WITH AND WITHOUT RETURNS

Having taken into consideration all the factors contributing to the lateral strength of the wall, an approximate analysis† can be developed based on the following assumptions:

i)   Elastic deflections of the wall supports are negligible

ii) Failure occurs by horizontal cracking at the top, centre, and bottom of the wall, causing rotation about horizontal lines through A, B and C (Fig. 7.4).

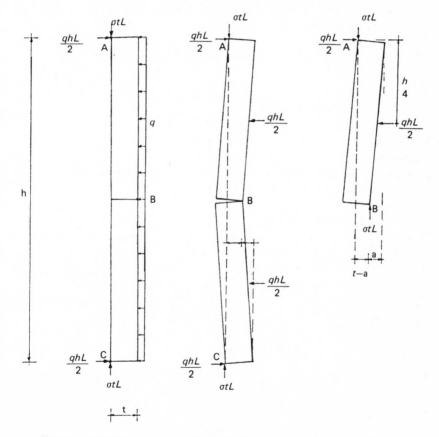

Fig. 7.4 – Simplified failure mechanism of walls supported top and bottom
q Lateral pressure σ Precompressive stress L Length of wall.

† Hendry, A. W., Sinha, B. P. and Maurenbrecher, A. H. P., 'Full-scale tests on the lateral strength of brick cavity-walls without precompression', *Proceedings of 4th Symposium on Loadbearing Brickwork,* British Ceramic Society, Stoke-on-Trent 1971, 141–164.

The forces acting on the top half of the wall at the point of failure are shown in Fig. 7.4. By taking moments about A

$$\sigma t L(t - a) = q_0 \, hL/2 \cdot h/4 \tag{7.1}$$

$$q_0 = 8\sigma t (t - a)/h^2 \tag{7.2}$$

where σ = precompressive stress, t = thickness of the wall which is subjected to precompression (in the case of a cavity wall with inner-leaf loaded, thickness should be equal to the thickness of inner leaf only), L = length of wall, h = height wall, q_0 = transverse or lateral pressure, a = horizontal distance through which centre of the wall has moved.

If the compressive stress is assumed constant throughout the uplift of the wall at failure, the maximum pressure resisted by the wall is equal to:

$$q_0 = \frac{8\sigma t^2}{h^2} \text{ when } a = 0. \tag{7.3}$$

If the precompression increases on the wall with uplift of the building, as explained above, it is possible for the moment of resistance, $\sigma \, tl \, (t - a)$, to increase, even though the moment arm $(t - a)$ decreases – thus resulting in an increase in the maximum lateral pressure resisted by the wall.

7.3.1 Wall with returns
In the case of a wall with returns, part of the lateral pressure is transmitted to the return, thus causing axial and bending stresses in the return. In simplified analysis, however, the return is assumed not to fail. The lateral pressure transmitted to the return is assumed to be distributed over the height of the wall at 45° (Fig. 7.5). Considering a wall with one return and taking the moment of all the forces acting on the top half of the wall (Fig. 7.5) about the top:

$$\sigma t^2 L = q_1 \frac{h}{2} \, L \cdot h/4 \; - \; q_1 h^2/8 \cdot h/3 \tag{7.4}$$

therefore $\quad q_1 = \dfrac{8\sigma t^2}{h^2} \cdot \dfrac{1}{1 - 1/3\alpha}$ where $\alpha = L/h \geqslant 0.5$. $\tag{7.5}$

Now substituting the value of q_0 (wall with no return) from equation (7.3) to equation (7.5)

$$q_1 = q_0 \cdot \frac{1}{1 - 1/3\alpha} \tag{7.6}$$

similarly, for a wall with two returns, Fig. 7.5(a),

$$\sigma t^2 L = q_2 \frac{hL}{2} \cdot h/4 - q_2 h^2/8 \cdot \frac{2h}{3} \tag{7.7}$$

$$q_2 = \frac{8 t^2}{h^2} \cdot \frac{1}{1 - 2/3\alpha} \quad \text{where} \quad \alpha = L/h \geqslant 1 . \tag{7.8}$$

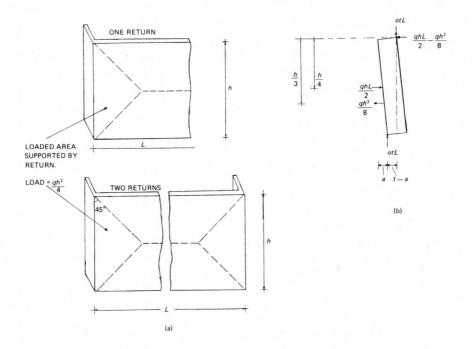

Fig. 7.5 – Simplified failure mechanism for walls with returns.

From equation (7.3)

$$q_2 = q_0 . \; 1/(1 - 2/3\alpha) \tag{7.9}$$

for various values of α, the q_1/q_0 and q_2/q_0 have been shown in Fig. 7.6 together with the experimental results.

In the British Code of Practice 5628 the factors, $1/(1 - 1/3\alpha)$ and $1/(1 - 2/3\alpha)$ are replaced by a single factor k. Table 7.1 shows the comparison between factor k obtained from the theory and from the Code.

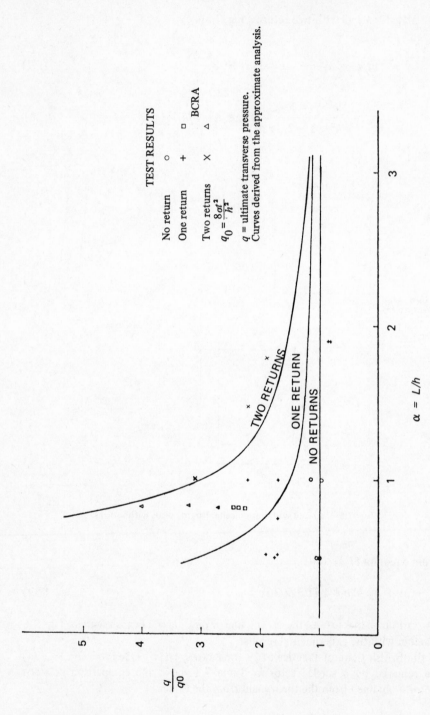

Fig. 7.6 – Effect of returns on the lateral strength of walls with varying L/h ratios

Table 7.1 Comparison of the value k

Number of returns	Value of k			
	$L/h = 0.75$	1.0	2.0	3.0
1	1.6(1.8)	1.5(1.5)	1.1(1.2)	1.0(1.1)
2	4.0(–)	3.0(3.1)	1.5(1.5)	1.2(1.28)

NOTE: Theoretical values in brackets.

From Table 7.1 it can be seen that the British Code values are in good agreement with the theoretical results. The theoretical values in some cases have been slightly adjusted in the light of experimental results which are shown in Fig. 7.6. Because of the simplified assumption that the return will not fail before the wall, the curves (Fig. 7.6) for q_1/q_0 and q_2/q_0 at lower L/h ratio become asymptotic to the Y-axis which is physically not possible, hence the Code has used a cut-off point on the evidence of experimental results.

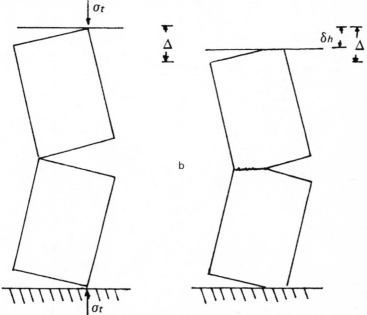

Fig. 7.7 – Effect of wall rotation. (a) basic rotation, (b) modified rotation (with high precompression).
σ = Precompression
Δ = Half maximum uplift of wall with no corner deformations
δ_h = Elastic shortening

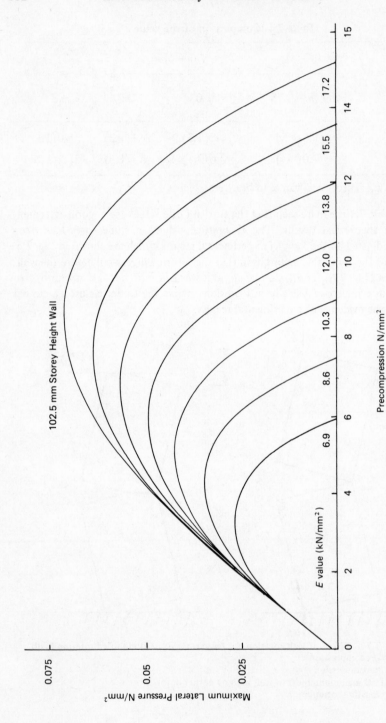

Fig. 7.8 – Precompression *v*. Maximum Lateral Pressure 102.5 mm wall of storey height.

7.4 EFFECT OF VERY HIGH PRECOMPRESSION

From equation (7.3) it can be seen that the lateral pressure varies directly with precompression; this is perfectly true for an ideal rigid body. In brick walls with high precompression, as the two blocks rotate (Fig. 7.7) on top of each other resulting in a reduced effective cross-sectional area with very high local stress approaching ultimate strength in crushing, the failure will be earlier than predicted by the straight-line theory of equation (7.3). At a precompression equal to the ultimate strength of brickwork, the wall will fail without resisting any lateral pressure. From Fig. 7.8, which has been derived analytically taking into account the deformation of the wall, it can be seen that the maximum capacity of resisting lateral pressure for any strength of brickwork is reached at a precompression equal to approximately half of the ultimate strength. After this value of precompression, the lateral load-resisting capacity of a wall decreases. As the design stress in compression utilises only a fraction of the ultimate brickwork strength and will never exceed half of the ultimate strength, in almost all practical cases the failure condition will be in the linear range of Fig. 7.8; hence the simplified approximate analysis can accurately and safely be applied.

7.5 LATERAL LOAD DESIGN OF PANELS WITHOUT PRECOMPRESSION

Brickwork panels which resist out-of-plane lateral loading may be supported as follows:

i)   Simply supported top and bottom, i.e. vertically spanning panel

ii) Simply supported on two edges, i.e. horizontally spanning panel

iii) Simply supported or continuous on three or four sides, i.e. panels supported on more than two sides of various boundary conditions.

It will of course be realised that simple supports are an idealisation of actual conditions which will usually be capable of developing some degree of moment resistance.

7.5.1 Vertically or horizontally spanning panels
The maximum moments per unit width for wall spanning vertically or horizontally can be calculated from:

Vertically spanning panel $M_y = wh^2/8$ (7.10)

Horizontally spanning panel $M_x = wL^2/8$ (7.11)

where w = design pressure, M_x and M_y = maximum moments per unit width at mid-span on strips of unit width and span h and L.

Similarly, the moment of resistance per unit width of the panel can be calculated from the known value of the flexural tensile strengths in respective directions as:

$$M_y = f_{ty} Z \tag{7.12}$$

where f_{ty} = allowable tensile strength $\perp$ to the bed joint

$$M_x = f_{tx} \cdot Z \tag{7.13}$$

where f_{tx} = allowable tensile strength $/\!/$ to the bed joint

Z = sectional modulus for unit width   .

In case of limit state design, the design bending moments per unit width in two directions will be

$$M_y = w_k \gamma_f h^2 / 8 \quad (7.14) \text{ where } w_k - \text{characteristic wind load per unit area}$$

$$M_x = w_k \gamma_f L^2 / 8 \quad (7.15) \qquad \gamma_f - \text{partial safety factor for loads}$$

The moment of resistance of the panel spanning vertically and horizontally will be given by

$$M_y = \frac{f_{ky} \cdot Z}{\gamma_m} \tag{7.16}$$

$$M_x = \frac{f_{kx}}{\gamma_m} \cdot Z \quad \text{where } f_{ky} \text{ and } f_{kx} \text{ characteristic tensile strength normal and} \\ \text{parallel to bedjoints} \tag{7.17}$$

7.5.2 Panels supported on more than two sides with various boundary conditions

The lateral load analysis of brickwork panels of various boundary conditions is very complicated since brickwork has different strength and stiffness properties in two orthogonal directions. Typical values of brickwork moduli of elasticity on which the stiffness depends are given in Table 7.2.

The new British limit-state code BS 5628 recommends bending moment co-efficients for the design of laterally loaded panels. The code does not indicate the origin of these coefficients, but they are numerically equal to those given by yield-line analysis as applied to under-reinforced concrete slab with corresponding boundary conditions. Strictly speaking, yield-line analysis is not applicable to a brittle material like brickwork which cannot develop constant-moment hinges as occur in reinforced concrete with yielding of the steel. It is not surprising, therefore, that a comparison between test results and those derived from yield-line analysis show that the yield-line method consistently overestimates the failure pressure when the orthogonal ratio for brickwork is interpreted as the strength ratio. Since brickwork panels exhibit different strengths and stiffness properties in two orthogonal directions, a simplified method for the design based on fracture lines taking into account both strength and stiffness orthotropies is discussed below. The method has been applied to predict the failure pressure of rectangular panels, rectangular panels with opening, octogonal and and triangular panels of various boundary conditions, and may be used for the design of brickwork panels using the published values of the stiffness orthotropy and flexural strengths.

Table 7.2 Moduli of elasticity of brickwork in two orthogonal directions
(Grade I and II mortar)

Type of brick	Modulus of elasticity of brickwork	
	E_y kN/mm^2	E_x kN/mm^2
Single frog (low strength 21.55 N/mm^2)	6.2	8.8
Double frog (Medium strength 59.40 N/mm^2)	8.65	15.3
Three holes perforated (high strength 88.33 N/mm^2)	18.13	16.53

7.5.3 Fracture line analysis[†]
The fracture line analysis which is described here is an ultimate load design method for laterally loaded panels.

Assumptions
All deformations take place along the fracture lines only, and the individual parts of the slab rotate as rigid bodies. The load distribution is in accordance with the stiffnesses in the respective directions. The fracture lines develop only when the relevant strengths are reached in two directions.

[†] Sinha, B. P., 'A simplified ultimate load analysis of laterally loaded model orthotropic brickwork panels of low tensile strength', *The Structural Engineer*, Dec. 1978, Vo. 50B, No. 4, 81–84.
Sinha, B. P., 'An ultimate load analysis of laterally loaded brickwork panels', *The International Jounral of Masonry Construction*, Vol. 1, No. 2, 1980, 57–61.

Consider the idealised fracture lines for a four-sided panel with two simply supported and two continuous edges (see Fig. 7.9). Every portion of the panel into which it is divided by the fracture lines is in equilibrium under the action of external forces and reaction along the fracture lines and supports. Since it is symmetrical, only parts 1 and 2 need consideration.

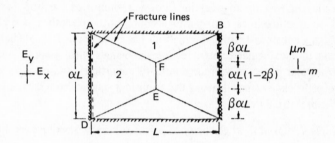

Fig. 7.9 — Idealised fracture lines.

In case of asymmetry the entire rigid area needs to be considered.

The load on $AFB(1) = \frac{1}{2} w\beta\alpha L^2$ and its moment $\qquad$ (7.18)

along $\quad$ AB $\quad = \frac{1}{2} w\beta\alpha L^2 \times (\beta\alpha L/3)$ [Since CG of load drops $\frac{1}{3}$]

$\qquad\qquad = w\beta^2\alpha^2 L^3/6 \qquad$ (7.19)

For equilibrium $\quad w\beta^2\alpha^2 L^3/6 = mL$, therefore
$$w\beta\alpha^2 L^2/6 = m/\beta \ . \qquad (7.20)$$

Similarly, the AFED(2) (The left hand of equation has been obtained by dividing the rigid body 2 into two triangles and one rectangle for simplification of the calculation)

$$(wL^2\beta/12) + (wL^2/8) - (wL^2\beta/4) = 2\mu m/K \text{ where } K = E_x/E_y \qquad (7.21)$$

or $\qquad (wL^2/12) \, [\beta + 1.5 - 3\beta] = 2\mu m/K$

or $\qquad (w\alpha^2 L^2/6) \, [1.5 - 2\beta] = 4\mu m\alpha^2/K \ .$

From equations (7.20) and (7.21),

$$(w\alpha^2 L^2/6) \, [1.5 - 2\beta + \beta] = (m/\beta) + (4\mu m\alpha^2/K) \qquad (7.22)$$

or $(w\alpha^2 L^2/6) [1.5 - \beta] = (m/\beta) [1 + (4\mu\beta\alpha^2/K)]$, therefore

$$m = \frac{w\alpha^2 L^2}{6} \left[\frac{1.5\beta - \beta^2}{1 + (4\mu\beta\alpha^2/K)} \right]. \tag{7.23}$$

For minimum collapse load or maximum value of moment d $(m/w)/d\beta = 0$,

from which $\beta = \dfrac{K}{4\mu\alpha^2} \left[\sqrt{\dfrac{6\mu\alpha^2}{K} + 1} \; - \; 1 \right]$ | (7.24)

The value of β can be substituted in equations to obtain the relationship between the failure moment and the load.

For a particular panel, the fracture pattern that gives the lowest collapse load should be taken as failure load. The values of m and β for various fracture line patterns for panels of different boundary conditions are given in Table 7.3, and the reader can derive them from first principles as explained above.

7.5.4 How to obtain the bending moment coefficient of BS 5628 from the fracture line analysis

Although the fracture line method has been suggested for accurate analysis, the designer may prefer to use the BS 5628 coefficients, hence this section briefly outlines the method to obtain the coefficients from the fracture-line. In BS 5628 the bending moment coefficients are given for horizontal bending (M_x), whereas the analysis presented in this chapter considers the vertical bending (M_y). Similarly, the orthotropy ratio in case of BS 5628 is taken as the ratio of $\dfrac{\text{strength} \perp \text{to bedjoint,}}{\text{strength} \, / \! / \, \text{to bedjoint}}$ hence orthotropy is less than 1, whereas in the present analysis the orthotropy is the reciprocal of this ratio.

The BS 5628 coefficients can be obtained by putting $K = 1$ in equations (7.24) and (7.23) and also in the equation of Appendix A, and by multiplying the vertical moment m (M_y) by the orthotropy defined as in the fracture line analysis.

Example.
Consider a case of panel similar to Fig. 7.8.

$$\mu = \frac{\text{strength} \, / \! / \, \text{to bedjoint}}{\text{strength} \perp \text{to bedjoint}} = 3.33 \quad \alpha = h/L = 0.75$$

(*Note:* In BS 5628 the symbol α is used for bending moment coefficient).

Table 7.3 Ultimate bending moment for panels of different boundary conditions.

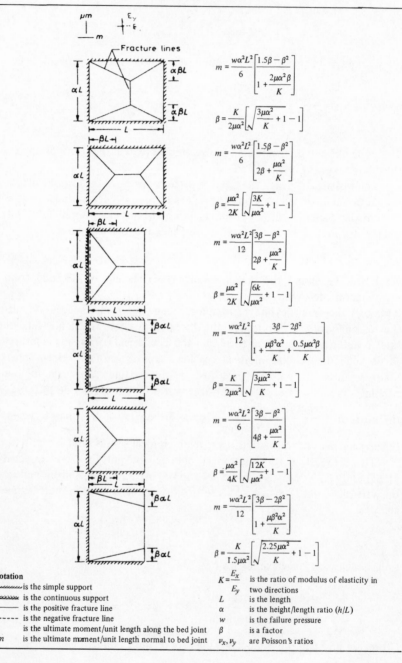

$$m = \frac{w\alpha^2 L^2}{6}\left[\frac{1.5\beta - \beta^2}{1 + \dfrac{2\mu\alpha^2\beta}{K}}\right]$$

$$\beta = \frac{K}{2\mu\alpha^2}\left[\sqrt{\frac{3\mu\alpha^2}{K} + 1} - 1\right]$$

$$m = \frac{w\alpha^2 L^2}{6}\left[\frac{1.5\beta - \beta^2}{2\beta + \dfrac{\mu\alpha^2}{K}}\right]$$

$$\beta = \frac{\mu\alpha^2}{2K}\left[\sqrt{\frac{3K}{\mu\alpha^2} + 1} - 1\right]$$

$$m = \frac{w\alpha^2 L^2}{12}\left[\frac{3\beta - \beta^2}{2\beta + \dfrac{\mu\alpha^2}{K}}\right]$$

$$\beta = \frac{\mu\alpha^2}{2K}\left[\sqrt{\frac{6k}{\mu\alpha^2} + 1} - 1\right]$$

$$m = \frac{w\alpha^2 L^2}{12}\left[\frac{3\beta - 2\beta^2}{1 + \dfrac{\mu\beta^2\alpha^2}{K} + \dfrac{0.5\mu\alpha^2\beta}{K}}\right]$$

$$\beta = \frac{K}{2\mu\alpha^2}\left[\sqrt{\frac{3\mu\alpha^2}{K} + 1} - 1\right]$$

$$m = \frac{w\alpha^2 L^2}{6}\left[\frac{3\beta - \beta^2}{4\beta + \dfrac{\mu\alpha^2}{K}}\right]$$

$$\beta = \frac{\mu\alpha^2}{4K}\left[\sqrt{\frac{12K}{\mu\alpha^2} + 1} - 1\right]$$

$$m = \frac{w\alpha^2 L^2}{12}\left[\frac{3\beta - 2\beta^2}{1 + \dfrac{\mu\beta^2\alpha^2}{K}}\right]$$

$$\beta = \frac{K}{1.5\mu\alpha^2}\left[\sqrt{\frac{2.25\mu\alpha^2}{K} + 1} - 1\right]$$

Notation

⌁⌁⌁⌁ is the simple support	
✕✕✕✕ is the continuous support	
——— is the positive fracture line	
- - - - - is the negative fracture line	
m is the ultimate moment/unit length along the bed joint	
μm is the ultimate moment/unit length normal to bed joint	

$K = \dfrac{E_x}{E_y}$ is the ratio of modulus of elasticity in two directions

L is the length
α is the height/length ratio (h/L)
w is the failure pressure
β is a factor
ν_x, ν_y are Poisson's ratios

From equation (7.24)

$$= \frac{K}{4\mu\alpha^2} \left[\sqrt{\frac{6\mu\alpha^2}{K} + 1} \; -1 \right]$$

$$= \frac{1}{4 \times 3.33 \times (0.75)^2} \left[\sqrt{\frac{6 \times 3.33 \times (.75)^2}{1} + 1} \; -1 \right] = 0.3334 \quad .$$

From equation (7.23) vertical moment

$$m = \frac{w\alpha^2 L^2}{6} \left[\frac{1.5\beta - \beta^2}{1 + 4\mu\beta\alpha^2/K} \right]$$

$$= \frac{wL^2}{6} \times (0.75)^2 \left[\frac{1.5 \times 0.3334 - (0.3334)^2}{1 + \dfrac{4 \times 3.33 \times 0.3334 \times (0.75)^2}{1}} \right] = 0.0104wL^2,$$

therefore horizontal moment

$$\mu m = 0.0104 \times 3.33wL^2 = 0.035wL^2 \quad .$$

The bending moment coefficient from **BS** 5628 for corresponding case ($h/L = 0.75$); is also 0.035.

CHAPTER 8

Composite Action between Walls and other Elements

8.1 COMPOSITE WALL BEAMS

8.1.1 Introduction

If a wall and the beam on which it is supported can be considered to act as a single composite unit then, for design purposes, the proportion of the load acting on the wall which is carried by the supporting beam must be determined. Prior to 1952 it was common practice to design the beams or lintels so as to be capable of carrying a triangular load of brickwork in which the span of the beam represented the base of an equilateral triangle. The method allowed for a proportion of the self weight of the brickwork but ignored any additional superimposed load.

Since that period a great deal of research, both practical and theoretical, has been undertaken, and a better understanding of the problem is now possible.

Consider the simply supported wall beam shown in Fig. 8.1. The action of the load introduces tensile forces in the beam due to the bending of the deep composite wall beam and, since the beam now acts as a tie, the supports are partially restrained horizontally so that an arching action results in the panels. The degree of arching is dependent on the relative stiffness of the wall to the beam, and it will be shown later that both the flexural stiffness and the axial stiffness must be taken into account. In general, the stiffer the beam the greater the beam-bending moment since a larger proportion of the load will be transmitted to the beam.

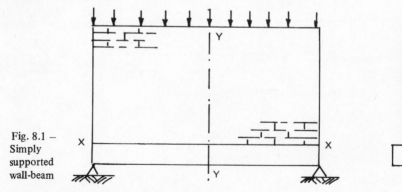

Fig. 8.1 – Simply supported wall-beam

The values of the vertical and horizontal stresses depend on a number of factors, but typical plots of the vertical and horizontal stress distributions along XX and YY of Fig. 8.1 are shown in Fig. 8.2.

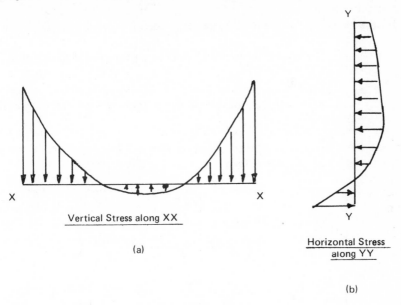

Vertical Stress along XX

(a)

Horizontal Stress along YY

(b)

Fig. 8.2 — Stress distribution.

Note that the maximum vertical stress, along the wall/beam interface, occurs at the supports and that at mid-span the horizontal stresses in the beam may be tensile throughout the depth so that the beam acts as a tie.

Composite action cannot be achieved unless there is sufficient bond between the wall and the beam to allow for the development of the required shearing forces. The large compressive stresses near the supports result in large frictional forces along the interface, and it has been shown that if the depth/span ratio of the wall is > 0.6 then the frictional forces developed are sufficient to supply the required shear capacity.

8.1.2 Development of Design Methods

For design purposes the quantities which must be determined are:

1. The maximum vertical stress in the wall.

2. The axial force in the beam.

3. The maximum shear stress along the interface.

4. The central bending moment in the beam.

5. The maximum bending moment in the beam and its location.

In 1952 methods which allowed for arching action, were developed for determining the bending moment and axial force in the beams. The panels were assumed to have a depth/span ratio greater than 0.6 so that the necessary relieving arch action could be developed and moment coefficients were introduced to enable the beam-bending moments to be determined. These were:

$\dfrac{PL}{100}$ for plain walls or walls with door or window openings occurring at centre span

$\dfrac{PL}{50}$ for walls with door or window openings occurring near the supports.

An alternative approach, based on the assumption that the moment arm between the centres of compression and tension was $\frac{2}{3} \times$ overall depth with a limiting value of $0.7 \times$ the wall span (Fig. 8.3), was also suggested.

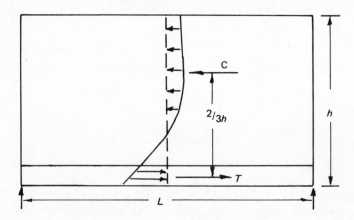

Fig. 8.3 – Moment capacity of wall-beam.

Using this assumption, the tensile force in the beam can be calculated using

$$T \times \tfrac{2}{3}h = PL/8 \qquad (8.1)$$

and the beam designed to carry this force.

Following this early work of Wood and Simms, the composite wall beam problem was studied by a number of researchers who considered not only the design of the beam but also the stresses in the wall. The characteristic parameter K introduced by Stafford-Smith to express the relative stiffness of the wall and beam was shown to be a useful parameter for the determination of both the compressive stresses in the wall and the bending moments in the beam. The value of K is given by

$$K = \sqrt[4]{(E_w t L^3 / E_{bm} I_b)} \tag{8.2}$$

where E_w and E_{bm} = Young's moduli of the wall and beam respectively

$\quad I_b$ = Second moment of area of the beam

$\quad t, L$ = Wall thickness and span .

The parameter K does not contain the variable h since it was considered that the ratio of h/L was equal to 0.6 and that this was representative of walls for which the actual h/L value was greater.

Conservative estimates of the stresses in walls on beam structures with restrained or free ends based on the above are,

Maximum moment in beam $= PL/4(E_w t L^3 / E_{bm} I_b)^{\frac{1}{3}} \tag{8.3}$

Maximum tie force in beam $= P/3.4 \tag{8.4}$

Maximum stress in wall $= 1.63(P/Lt)(E_w t L^3 / E_{bm} I_b)^{0.28} \tag{8.5}$

Note that assuming $h/L = 0.6$, equation (8.1) above becomes $T = P/3.2$ which is similar to equation (8.4).

In 1980 an approximate method of analysis based on a graphical approach was introduced. This method is described in the next section.

8.1.3 Basic Assumptions

The walls considered are built of brickwork or blockwork and the beams of concrete or steel. It is assumed that there is sufficient bond between the wall and the beam to carry the shear stress at the interface, and this presupposes that a steel beam would be encased and the ratio of h/L would be $\geqslant 0.6$.

The loading, including the self weight of the wall, is represented by a distributed load along the top surface. Care must be taken with additional loads placed at beam level since the tensile forces that might result could destroy the composite action by reducing the frictional resistance.

Two stiffness parameters, R and K_1, are introduced to enable the appropriate stresses and moments to be determined. The first is a flexural stiffness parameter similar to that introduced by Stafford-Smith except that height of the wall replaces the span and the second an axial stiffness parameter used for determining the axial force in the beam.

$$R = \sqrt[4]{E_w t h^3 / E_{bm} I_b} \tag{8.6}$$

$$K_1 = E_w t h / E_{bm} A_b . \tag{8.7}$$

A typical vertical stress distribution at the wall-beam interface is shown in Fig. 8.2(a). To simplify the analysis it is assumed that the distribution of this stress can be represented by a straight line, a square parabola or a cubic parabola depending on the range of R as shown in Fig. 8.4.

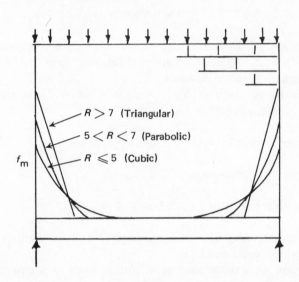

Fig. 8.4 – Vertical stress distribution.

The axial force in the beam is assumed to be linear with a maximum value at the centre and zero at the supports.

8.1.4 The Graphical Method

8.1.4.1 *Maximum Vertical Stress in Wall* (f_m)

This stress is a maximum over the supports and can be determined using the equation

$$f_m = (P/Lt)C_1 \qquad (8.8)$$

where C_1 can be obtained from Fig. 8.5 using the calculated values of R and h/L.

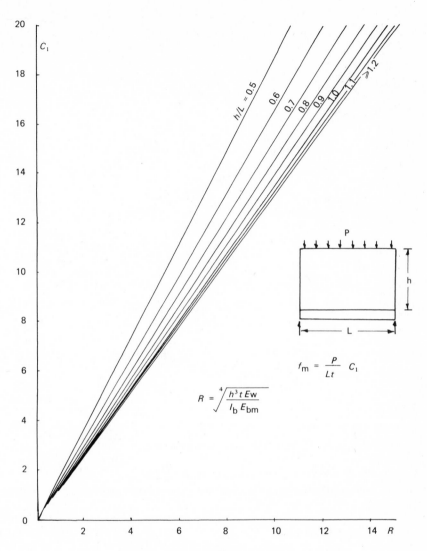

Fig. 8.5 – Flexural stiffness parameter.

8.1.4.2 *Axial force in the beam* (T)

This force is assumed to be a maximum at the centre and can be determined using the equation

$$T = PC_2 \tag{8.9}$$

where C_2 can be found from Fig. 8.6 using the calculated values of K_1 and h/L.

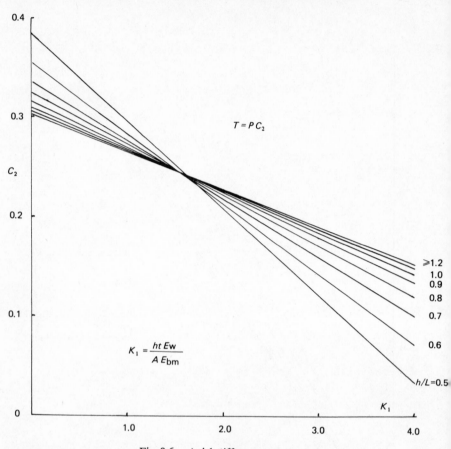

Fig. 8.6 — Axial stiffness parameter.

8.1.4.3 *Maximum Shear Stress along Interface* (τ_m)

The maximum interface shear occurs near the supports and can be determined using,

$$\tau_m = (P/Lt)\, C_1 C_2 \qquad\qquad (8.10)$$

where C_1 and C_2 are the values already obtained from Figs. 8.5 and 8.6.

8.1.4.4 *Bending Moments in the beam*

The maximum bending moment in the beam does not occur at the centre, because of the influence of the shear stresses along the interface. Both the maximum and central bending moments can, however, be obtained from one graph (for a particular range of R) by using the appropriate abscissae. The three graphs, Figs. 8.7, 8.8, 8.9 have been drawn so that each represents a relationship for the particular range of R shown.

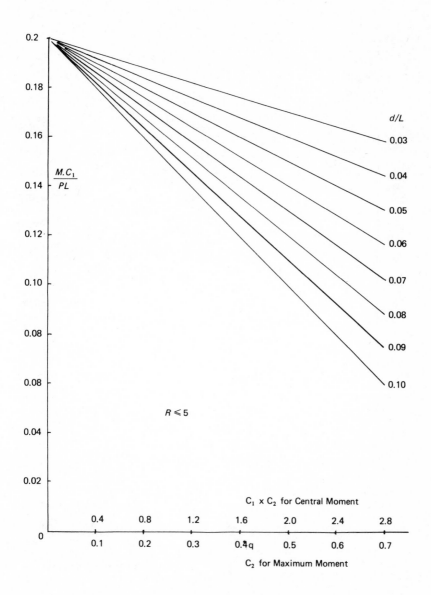

Fig. 8.7 – Moments for triangular stress distribution.

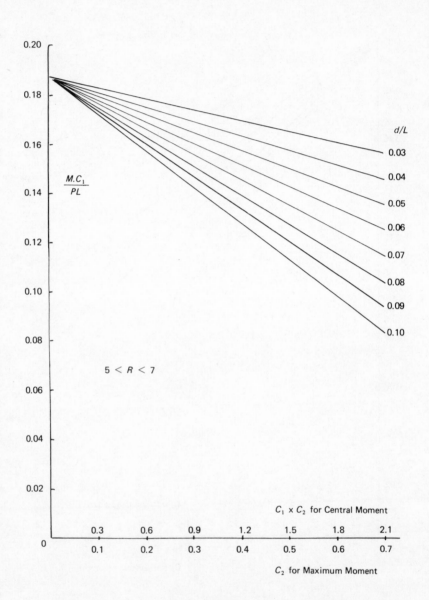

Fig. 8.8 – Moments for parabolic stress distribution.

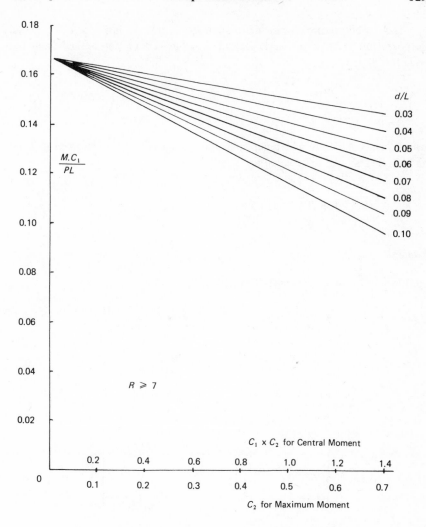

Fig. 8.9 – Moments for cubic stress distribution.

To obtain the maximum moment, the lower C_2 scale is used and for the central moment the C_1. C_2 scale is used. In each case use of the appropriate d/L ratio will give the value of

$$M.C_1/PL \qquad (8.11)$$

where M is either the maximum or the central bending moment.

The location of the maximum moment is not so important for design purposes but if required an approximate value can be determined from the equation,

$$l = \frac{P}{2S \cdot f_m \cdot t} \tag{8.12}$$

where S is a coefficient which depends on the shape of the vertical stress diagram and can be assumed to be equal to

0.30 for $R \leqslant 5$,

0.33 for R between 5 and 7,

0.5 for $R \geqslant 7$

Example

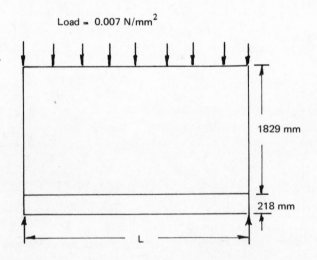

Fig. 8.10 – Dimensions for wall-beam example. $L = 2743$ mm, $b = t = 115$ mm.

To illustrate the use of the method consider the wall-beam shown in Fig. 8.10.

$$E_{bm}/E_w = 30 \qquad I_b = 115 \times 218^3/12$$

$$= 9.93 \times 10^7 \, mm^4$$

$$R = (1829^3 \times 115 \times 1)/(9.93 \times 10^7 \times 30) = 236.23$$

$$= 3.92$$

$$K_1 \doteq (1829 \times 115)/(30 \times 115 \times 218) = 0.28$$

$$h/L = 1829/2743 = 0.67$$

$$d/L = 218/2743 = 0.079$$

Total load $= 0.007 \times 2743 \times 115 = 2208$ N

Using the graphs, $C_1 = 6.8$ and $C_2 = 0.325$, therefore

$$f_m = \frac{2208}{2743 \times 115} \times 6.8 = 0.0476 \text{ N/mm}^2$$

$$T = 2208 \times 0.325 = 717.6 \text{ N}$$

$$\tau_m = \frac{2208}{2743 \times 115} \times 6.8 \times 0.325 = 0.0155 \text{ N/mm}^2$$

From Fig. 8.7, $M_c C_1/PL = 0.115$ and $M_m C_1/PL = 0.144$

where M_c = centre line moment

and M_m = maximum moment,

or $$M_c = \frac{0.115 \times 2208 \times 2743}{6.8} = 1.02 \times 10^5 \text{ Nmm}$$

$$M_m = \frac{0.144 \times 2208 \times 2743}{6.8} = 1.28 \times 10^5 \text{ Nmm}$$

Location of max. moment from support $= 2208/(2 \times 0.3 \times 0.48 \times 115)$ $= 66.67$ mm.

These calculations are carried out in terms of design loads and are to be compared with the design strengths of the material in compression and shear. The design of the beam would be carried out in accordance with the relevant code of practice.

8.2 INTERACTION BETWEEN WALL PANELS AND FRAMES

8.2.1 Introduction
Wall panels built into frameworks of steel or reinforced concrete contribute to the overall stiffness of the structure, and a method is required for predicting modes of failure and calculating stresses and lateral collapse loads.

The problem has been studied by a number of authors, and although methods of solution have been proposed, work is still continuing and more laboratory or field testing is required to verify the proposed theoretical approaches.

A theoretical analysis based on a fairly sophisticated finite element approach which allowed for cracking within the elements as the load was increased was used by Stafford–Smith and Riddington. An alternative method developed by Wood was based on idealised plastic failure modes and then applying a correcting factor to allow for the fact that masonry is not ideally plastic.

These methods are too cumbersome for practical design purposes, and simplifying assumptions are made for determining acceptable approximate values of the unknowns.

The basis of the design method proposed by Stafford–Smith† is that the framed panel, in shear, acts as a diagonal strut, and failure of the panel occurs owing to compression in the diagonal or shear along the bedding planes. The beams and columns of the frame are designed on the basis of a simple static analysis of an equivalent frame with pin-jointed connections in which panels are represented as diagonal pin-jointed bracing structs.

A description of the design method proposed by Wood is given below.

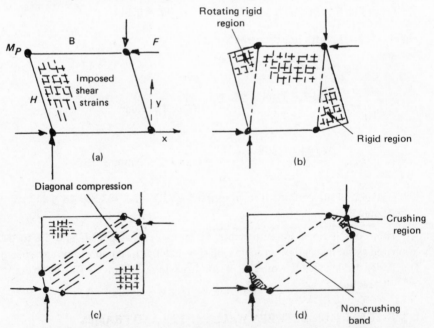

Fig. 8.11 – Idealized plastic failure modes for wall frame panels; (a) shear mode S (strong frame, weak wall), (b) shear rotation mode SR (medium strength walls), (c) diagonal compression mode DC (strong wall, weak frame), (d) corner crushing mode CC (very weak frame). (From Wood, Proc. of I.C.E., Vol. 65, 1978).

† The *Structural Engineer*, June 1977, No. 6, 55.

8.2.2. Design method based on plastic failure modes

8.2.2.1 *Introduction*

In the method proposed by Wood[††] four idealised plastic failure modes are considered, and these together with the loacation of plastic hinges are shown in Fig. 8.11.

A parameter m_d is introduced defined as

$$m_d = 8 \times M_p \cdot \gamma_m / (f_k tL^2) \tag{8.16}$$

where M_p is the lowest plastic moment of beams or columns, and f_k the characteristic strength of the masonry. This parameter which represents a frame/wall strength ratio is shown to be the factor which determines the mode of collapse.

For $m_d < 0.25$ the collapse mode is DC (Diagonal Compression) or CC (Corner Crushing)

For $0.25 < m_d < 1$ the collapse mode is SR (Shear Rotation)

For $m_d > 1$ the collapse mode is S (Shear)

8.2.2.2 *Design procedure*

(a) Initially the nominal value of m_d is calculated using equation (8.16) and then corrected using the factor δ_p obtained from Fig. 8.12. The corrected value (m_e) is given by $m_e = m_d / \delta_p$.

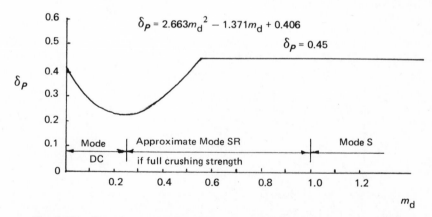

Fig. 8.12 – Plot of δ_p against m_d (from Wood, Proc. of I.C.E., Vol. 65, 1978).

(b) Calculate the value of the non-dimensional parameter ϕ_s using the equation

$$\phi_s = 2/(\sqrt{m_e} + 1/\sqrt{m_e}) \tag{8.17}$$

[††] *Proc. Institution Civil Engineers,* Part 2, 1978, 65, June.

This parameter was derived for square panels with identical beams and columns, and a correction factor Δ_ϕ must be determined for non-rectangular panels with unequal beams and columns, using Fig. 8.13 in which μ_p is defined as

$$\mu_p = \frac{\text{lowest beam plastic moment}}{\text{lowest column plastic moment}} \qquad (8.18)$$

If $\mu_p \geqslant 1$ (strong beams) use chart direct

If $\mu_p < 1$ (weak beams) and $L/h = 1$ use μ_p value in brackets

If $\mu_p < 1$ (weak beams) and $L/h > 1$ use $\mu_p = 1$ curve.

(c) Finally the design strength F can be determined using

$$F = \frac{(\phi_s + \Delta_\phi)}{1.2}\left(\frac{4(\text{smaller } M_p)}{h} + \tfrac{1}{2}\delta_p f_k \, t \, L/\gamma_m\right) \qquad (8.19)$$

where the factor 1.2 is an additional factor of safety introduced by Wood for design purposes and M_p is the effective plastic moment given by $Z\sigma_y/\gamma_{ms}$. For design purposes the design strength must be equal to or greater than the design load as shown in Chapter 4.

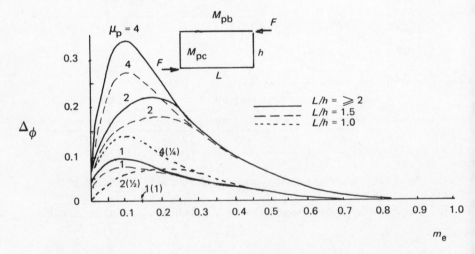

Fig. 8.13 — Design chart for racking loads: optional correction Δ_ϕ added to ϕ_s ($\mu = M_{pb}/M_{pc}$). (From Wood, Proc. of I.C.E., Vol. 65, 1978).

8.2.2.3 *Example*

Assume the following dimensions and properties

Panel height	— 2 m
Panel length	— 4 m
Panel thickness	— 110 mm

Characteristic strength of panel — 10 N/mm²

Partial safety factor for brickwork	— 3.1
Section modulus for each column	— 600 cm³
Section modulus for each beam	— 800 cm³
Yield stress of steel	— 250 N/mm²
Partial safety factor for steel	— 1.15

Effective plastic moment for beam = $(800 \times 10^3) \times 250/(1.15 \times 10^6)$

$$= 174 \text{ kN/m.}$$

Effective plastic moment for column $= 130 \text{ kN m,}$

$$\mu_p = 1.34,$$

$$L/h = 2 \quad .$$

$$m_d = \frac{8 \times 130 \times 10^6 \times 3.1}{10 \times 110 \times 4^2 \times 10^6} = 0.18 \quad .$$

From Fig. 8.12 $\delta_p = 0.25$

$$m_e = 0.24/0.25 = 0.96$$

$$\phi_s = \frac{2}{\sqrt{0.96} + 1/\sqrt{0.96}} = 1.0 \quad .$$

From Fig. 8.13 $\triangle_\phi = 0$

$$F = \frac{1.0}{1.2} \left(\frac{4 \times 130}{2} + \frac{0.25 \times (10/3.1) \times 110 \times 4000}{2 \times 10^3} \right)$$

$$= 217 \text{ (frame)} + 148 \text{ (wall)}$$

$$= 365 \text{ kN}$$

8.2.2.4 *Additional Considerations*

(a) A lower limiting sliding friction wall strength F_0 is defined for the wall if composite action fails or m_d is very low.

$$F_0 = L \, t \, f_v / \gamma_{mv}$$

where $f_v = 0.35 + 0.6 \, g_A \, \text{N/mm}^2$

$$f_v \not> 1.75 \quad . \tag{8.20}$$

for mortar designation (i) (ii) and (iii) and $f_v = 0.15 + 0.6 \, g_A$; $f_v \not> 1.4$ for mortar grade (iv) per unit area of wall cross-section due to the vertical dead and imposed load.

For the example given in 8.2.2.3, assuming mortar of grade (ii), f_v has minimum value of 0.35 (for no superimposed load) and a maximum value of 1.75. Therefore taking $\gamma_{mv} = 2.5$, F_0 has a value between 62 and 308 kN depending on the value of the superimposed load on the top beam.

(b) Design for shear in the columns and beams is based on

$$\text{Column shear} = \tfrac{1}{2} \, (F - F_0)$$

$$\text{Beam shear} = \tfrac{1}{2} \, (h/L) \, (F - F_0) \quad . \tag{8.21}$$

CHAPTER 9

Design for Accidental Damage

9.1 INTRODUCTION

It would be difficult to write about the effects of accidental damage to buildings without reference to the Ronan Point collapse which occurred in 1968. The progressive collapse of a corner of a 23-storey building caused by the accidental explosion of gas which blew out the external loadbearing flank wall and the non-loadbearing face walls of one of the flats on the 18th floor made designers aware that there was a weakness in a section of their design philosophy.

The Ronan Point building was constructed of large precast-concrete panels, and much of the initial concern related to structures of this type. However, it was soon realised that buildings constructed with other materials could also be susceptible to such collapse.

A great deal of research on brickwork structures was therefore carried out, leading to a better understanding of the problem. Research has been undertaken in many countries, and although differences in suggested methods for dealing with abnormal loadings still exist between countries there is also a lot of common ground, and acceptable design methods are now possible.

9.2 ACCIDENTAL LOADING

Accidental or abnormal loading can be taken to mean any loading which arises for which the structure is not normally designed. Two main cases can be identified 1) explosive loads, and 2) impact loads, but others could be added such as, settlement of foundations or structural alterations without due regard to safety.

Explosions can occur externally or internally and may be due to the detonation of a bomb, the ignition of a gas, or from transportation of an explosive chemical or gas. The pressure-time curves for each of these explosive types are different, and research has been carried out to determine the exact nature of each. However, although the loading caused by an explosion is of a dynamic nature, it is general practice to assume that they are static, and design checks are normally carried out on this basis.

Accidental impact loads can arise from highway vehicles or construction equipment. A motor vehicle could collide with a wall or column of a multi-storey building or a crane load accidentally impacted against a wall at any level. Both of these could cause collapse of a similar nature to those considered under explosive loading, but the method of dealing with the two types of loading may be different, as shown in section 9.4.

The risk of occurrence of an accidental load is obviously of importance in that certain risks, such as the risk of being struck by lightning, are acceptable whilst others are not. Designing for accidental damage adds to the overall cost of the building, and it is necessary to consider the degree of risk versus the increase in cost for proposed design methods to become acceptable.

The risks which society is prepared to accept can be compared numerically by considering the probability of death per person per annum for a series of types of accident. It is obvious that such estimates would vary both with time and geographical location, but values published for the United States based on accidental death statistics for the year 1966 are shown in Table 9.1.

Table 9.1

Motor vehicle	2.7×10^{-4}
Falling	1.0×10^{-4}
Fire	4.0×10^{-5}
Drowning	2.8×10^{-5}
Firearms	1.3×10^{-5}
Poisoning	1.1×10^{-5}
Earthquake	8.0×10^{-7}
Lightning	5.5×10^{-7}

Table 9.2

Explosive bombing	204
Gas explosions	131
Explosion of hazardous materials	177
Highway vehicle impact	190
Total/annum	702

It has also been shown that the risks for accidental damage is similar to that for fire and, since in the case of fire, design criteria are introduced there is a similar justification for adopting criteria to deal with accidental loading. The estimates for accidental damage were based on a study of the occurrence of abnormal loadings in the United States, and Table 9.2 shows a lower bound to the number of abnormal loadings per annum.

9.3 LIKELIHOOD OF OCCURRENCE OF PROGRESSIVE COLLAPSE

Accepting that accidental loading will occur it is necessary to consider the likelihood of such loading leading to progressive collapse.

A range of loadbearing brickwork buildings have been analysed, and basically there are three types of construction which required investigation in relation to accidental damage.

Case A, where there is an outside wall without returns or only one internal return (Fig. 9.1). Removal of a panel would leave the remaining section suspended on the floor slabs above.

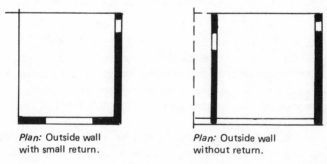

Plan: Outside wall
with small return.

Plan: Outside wall
without return.

Fig. 9.1 – Case A.

Case B, where there is an internal wall without return (Fig. 9.2). The walls above the damaged wall will have to be carried by the floor slab.

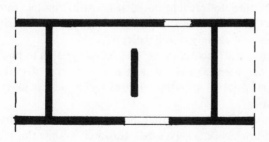

Fig. 9.2 – Case B.

Case C, where the removal of a section of a wall imposes high local bearing stresses on a return wall or walls (Fig. 9.3). Remaining brickwork is carried by return wall.

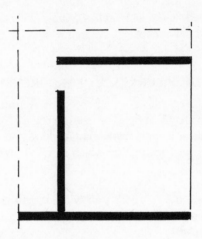

Fig. 9.3 – Case C.

An examination of a number of both high-rise (greater than six storeys) and low-rise structures for the possible occurrence of one of the above cases, followed by the removal of a panel and analysis of the remaining structure using the yield line theory, has shown that there would be little difficulty in designing brickwork buildings to satisfy the requirements in regard to partial collapse.

In addition, experimental tests have been conducted on a section of a five-storey brickwork cross-wall structure in which sections of the main cross walls of the ground floor were removed with a view to testing the stability of the structure in a damaged condition. The structure had not been specially designed to withstand such treatment but it remained stable throughout the tests, and it was concluded that there would be no difficulty in designing a brickwork structure to provide 'alternative paths' in the case of accidental damage. In fact, in many cases there would seem to be no necessity for additional elements to secure the safety of the structure.

The likelihood of occurrence of progressive collapse in buildings similar to Ronan Point has been considered, and it is estimated that the possibility of collapse is 0.045% i.e. 1 in every 2000 of such blocks is likely to collapse, in a life of 60 years.

In summary it would appear that the risk of progressive collapse in buildings of loadbearing brickwork is very small. However, against this the limited nature of the additional design precautions required to avoid such collapse are such that they add very little to the overall cost. In addition the social implications of failures of this type are great, and the collapse at Ronan Point will long be remembered. It added to the general public reaction against living in high-rise buildings.

9.4 POSSIBLE METHODS OF DESIGN

Design against progressive collapse could be introduced in two ways:

(a) Design against the occurrence of accidental damage.

(b) Allow accidental damage to occur and design against progressive collapse.

The first method would clearly be uneconomical in the general case, but it can be used to reduce the probability of local failure in certain cases. The risk of explosion, for example, could be reduced by restricting the use of gas in a building, and impact loads avoided by the design of suitable guards. However, reducing the probability does not eradicate the possibility, and progressive collapse could still occur so that most designers favour the second approach.

The second method implies that there should be a reasonable probability that progressive collapse will not occur in the event of a local failure. Obviously, all types of failure could not be catered for, and a decision has to be made as to the extent of allowable local failure to be considered. The extent of allowable local failure in an external wall may be greater than that for an internal wall and may be related to the number of storeys. Different countries tend to follow different rules with respect to this decision.

Having decided that local failure may occur it is now necessary to analyse the building to determine if there is a likelihood of progressive collapse. Three methods are available,

(a) A three-dimensional analysis of the structure.

(b) Two-dimensional analyses of sections taken through the building.

(c) A 'storey by storey' approach.

The first two methods require a finite element approach and are unsuitable for design purposes, although the results obtained from such realistic methods are invaluable for producing results which can lead to meaningful design procedures. A number of papers using this approach have been published, which allow not only for the nonlinear material effects but also dynamic loading.

The third approach is conservative in that having assumed the removal of a loadbearing element in a particular storey an assessment of residual stability is made from within that storey.

These theoretical methods of analysis together with experimental studies as mentioned in 9.3 have led to design recommendations as typified in BS 5628 (Section 9.6).

9.5 USE OF TIES

Codes of practice, such as BS 5628, require the use of ties as a means of limiting accidental damage. The provisions of BS 5628 in this respect have been summarised in Chapter 4.

The British Code distinguishes, in its recommendations for accidental damage design, between buildings of four storeys or less and those of five storeys or more. There are no special provisions for the first class, and there are three alternative options for the second (see Chapter 10).

It is convenient at this stage to list the types of ties used together with some of the design rules.

9.5.1 Vertical Ties

These may be wall or column ties and are continuous, apart from anchoring or lapping, from foundation to roof. They should be fully anchored at each end and at each floor level.

Note that since failure of vertical ties should be limited to the storey where the accident occurred it has been suggested that vertical ties should be independent in each storey height and should be staggered rather than continuous.

In BS 5628 the value of the tie force is given as,

$$T = (34A/8000) (h/t)^2 \, N \tag{9.1}$$

(or 100 kN/m length of wall or column, whichever is the greater)

  A = the horizontal cross-sectional area in mm^2 (excluding the non-load-bearing leaf of cavity construction but including piers)

  h = clear height of column or wall between restraining surfaces

  t = thickness of wall or column.

The code assumes that the minimum thickness of a solid wall or one load-bearing leaf of a cavity wall is 150 mm and that the minimum characteristic compressive strength of the masonry is 5 N/mm^2. Ties are positioned at a maximum of 5 m centres along the wall and 2.5 m max. from an unrestrained end of any wall. There is also a maximum limit of 25 on the ratio h/t in the case of narrow brick walls or 20 for other types of wall.

Example
Consider a cavity wall of length 5 m with an inner loadbearing leaf of thickness 170 mm and a total thickness 272 mm. Assume that the clear height between restraints is 3.0 m and that the characteristic steel strength is 250 N/mm^2.

Using equations (9.1)

$$\text{Tie force} = \frac{34}{8000} \times 5000 \times 170 \times \left(\frac{3000}{272}\right)^2 \times 10^3 = 439.5 \text{ kN}$$

or $100 \times 5 = 500$ kN

$$\text{Tie area} = \frac{500}{250} \times 10^3 = 2000 \text{ mm}^2 \text{ Use 7-20 mm diameter bars.}$$

This represents a steel percentage of $\dfrac{2000}{5000 \times 272} \times 100 = 0.15\%$.

9.5.2 Horizontal Ties

Horizontal ties are divided into four types and the design rules differ for each. There are (a) peripheral ties, (b) internal ties, (c) external wall ties, and (d) external column ties.

The basic horizontal tie force is defined as the lesser of the two values —

$$F_t = 20 + 4 N_s \text{ kN (where } N_s = \text{the number of storeys)}$$

$$\text{or} = 60 \text{ kN,} \tag{9.2}$$

but the actual value used varies with the type of tie (see below).

9.5.2.1 *Peripheral ties* are placed within 1.2 m of the edge of the floor or roof or in the perimeter wall. The tie force in kN is given by F_t from (9.2), and the ties should be anchored at re-entrant corners or changes of construction.

9.5.2.2 *Internal ties* are designed to span both ways and should be anchored to perimeter ties or continue as wall or column ties. In order to simplify the specification of the relevent tie force it is convenient to introduce F_t' such that

$$F_t' = F_t((G_k + Q_k)/7.5) \times L_a/5 \text{ (kN/m width)} \tag{9.3}$$

where $(G_k + Q_k)$ is the sum of the average characteristic dead and imposed loads in kN/m² and L_a is the lesser of:

(a) the greatest distance in metres in the direction of the tie, between the centres of columns or other vertical loadbearing members whether this distance is spanned by a single slab or by a system of beams and slabs, or

(b) 5 × clear storey height h (Fig. 9.4)

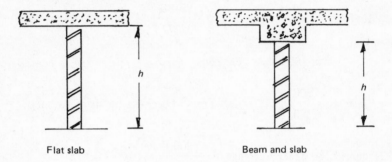

Flat slab   Beam and slab

Fig. 9.4 – Storey height.

The tie force in kN/m for internal ties is given as,

One-way slab
   In direction of span – greater value of F_t or F_t'

   Perpendicular to span – F_t .

Two-way slab
   In both directions – greater value of F_t or F_t' .

Internal ties are placed in addition to peripheral ties and are spaced uniformly throughout the slab width or concentrated in beams with a 6 m maximum horizontal tie spacing. Within walls they are placed at a maximum of 0.5 above or below the slab and at a 6 m maximum horizontal spacing.

9.5.2.3 *External wall or column ties*
The tie force for both external columns or walls is taken as the lesser value of $2F_t$ or $(h/2.5) F_t$ where h is in metres. For columns the force is in kN whilst in walls it is kN/m length of loadbearing wall.

Corner columns should be tied in both directions and the ties may be provided partly or wholly by the same reinforcement as perimeter and internal ties.

Wall ties should be spaced uniformly or concentrated at centres not more than 5 m apart and not more than 2.5 m from the end of the wall. They may be provided partly or wholly by the same reinforcement as perimeter and internal ties.

The tie force may be based on shear strength or friction as an alternative to steel ties (see examples).

9.5.2.4 Examples

Peripheral Ties
  For a 5-storey building
  the tie force = 20 + (5 × 4) = 40 kN
      Tie area = $(40 \times 10^3)/250 = 160$ mm^2
  Provide 1/15 mm bar within 1.2 m of edge of floor.

Internal Ties
  Assume $G_k = 5$ kN/m^2, $Q_k = 1.5$ kN/m^2 and $L_a = 4$ m

  $F_t = 40$ kN/m width
  $$F_t' = \frac{40(5 + 1.5)}{7.5} \times \frac{4}{5} = 35.5 \text{ kN/m width,}$$

therefore design for 40 kN/m both ways unless steel already provided as normal slab reinforcement.

External Wall Ties
  Assume clear storey height = 3.0 m

  Tie Force Either $2F_t = 80$ kN/m length,

  or $(h/2.5)F_t = (3.0/2.5) \times 40 = 48$ kN/m length (which governs).

  Shear Strength Using Clause 25,
      $f_v = 0.35 + 0.6g_A$ (or max. 1.75),
      or $= 0.15 + 0.6g_A$ (max. 1.4)
      depending on mortar strength.
      $\gamma_{mv} = 1.25$ from Clause 27.4.
      Assume mortar to be grade (i).

  Taking g_A, the design vertical load per unit area due to dead and imposed load, as zero, is conservative and equivalent to considering shear strength due to adhesion only. That is design shear strength on each surface $= f_v/\gamma_{mv} = 0.35/1.25 = 0.28$ N/mm^2,
  Combined resistance in shear on both surfaces
  = 2 × shear stress × area
  = 2 × 0.28 × (110 × 1000/1000) = 61.6 kN/m   .

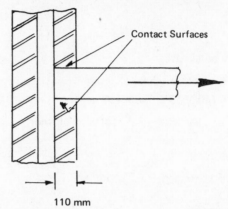

Fig. 9.5 – Surfaces providing frictional resistances.

In this example the required tie force of 48 kN/m is provided by the shear resistance of 61.6 kN/m, and additional steel ties are not required. If the shear resistance had been less than the required tie force, then the steel provided would be based on the full 48 kN/m.

Alternatively the required resistance may be provided by the frictional resistance at the contact surfaces. This calculation requires a knowledge of the dead loads from the floors and walls above the section being considered.

Assume dead loads as shown in Fig. 9.6. Using a coefficient of friction of 0.6 the total frictional resistance on surfaces A and B is $(20 + 10)0.6 + (20 + 10 + 18)0.6 = 46.8$ kN/m, which would be insufficient to provide the required tie force. Note that the code states that the calculation is based on shear strength or friction (but not both).

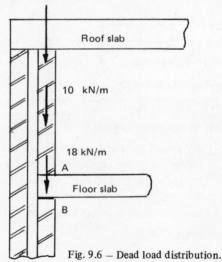

Fig. 9.6 – Dead load distribution.

CHAPTER 10

Design Calculations for a Seven-Storey Dormitory Building according to BS 5628

10.1 INTRODUCTION

As an illustration of structural design calculations based on BS 5628 we may consider a building having the layout shown in Fig. 10.1 and 10.2. It is assumed that the roof and floor slabs are of continuous 'in situ' reinforced concrete construction. The structure has been kept simple to show the principle of limit state design. Only two walls above G.L. – an internal wall A, heavily loaded compared to the others, and a cavity wall B, have been considered. The inner leaf is assumed to support its own weight together with roof and floor loads, whilst the outer leaf will support only its own weight. The design loads and design assumptions are given in section 10.2.

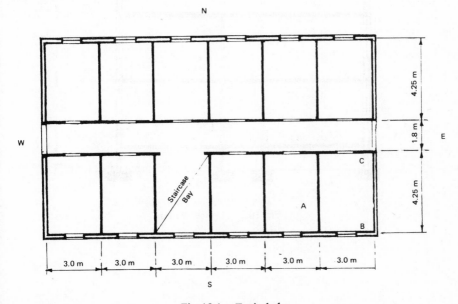

Fig. 10.1 – Typical plan.

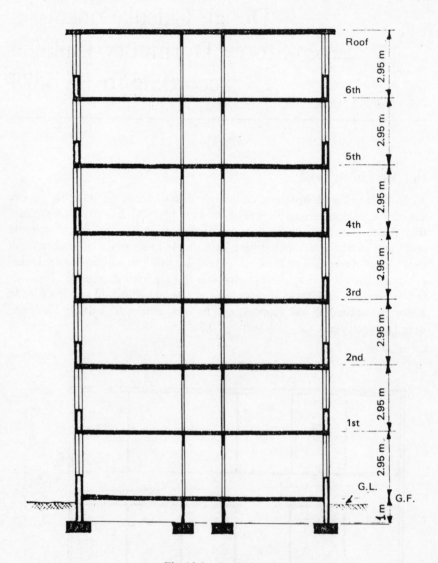

Fig. 10.2 – Typical section.

10.2 BASIS OF DESIGN

10.2.1 Loadings

Roof: Dead weight - 3.5 kN/m^2
        Imposed load - 1.5 kN/m^2

Floor: Dead weight including finishing and partition -- 4.8 kN/m^2
        Imposed load   - 1.5 kN/m^2

Wall: 102.5 mm with 13 mm plaster both sides   - 2.6 kN/m^2
        102.5 mm an inner skin of 255 mm cavity
        wall   - 2.42 kN/m^2
        (i.e. 102.5 mm + 1 face plaster)

Wind Load:
Speed (Edinburgh area) - 50 m/s

10.3 QUALITY CONTROL

Normal (factory and site)

10.3.1 Partial safety factors for materials

γ_m = 3.5 (Table 4, BS 5628)

γ_{mv} = 2.5 (Clause 27.4)

10.4 CALCULATION OF VERTICAL LOADING ON WALLS
Table 10.1 Loading on Wall A/m run.

Floor level considered	Load/m run (kN/m)		
	Dead at floor	Cumulative dead load to floor G_k	Cumulative live load to floor Q_k
6th floor: *dead wt.:* roof: 3.5 × 3 × 1.2* = 12.6 kN Wt. of wall: 2.6 × 2.85 = 7.4 kN 20.0 kN/m Imposed load: 1.5 × 3 × 1.2* = 5.4 kN/m	20.0	20.0	5.4
5th floor: *dead wt.:* Floor: 4.8 × 3 × 1.2* = 17.28 Wall: = 7.40 24.68 kN/m 90% of imposed load 2 × 5.4 × 0.9 = 9.72	24.68	44.68	9.72
4th floor: *dead wt.:* Floor; 4.8 × 3 × 1.2* = 17.28 Wall: 7.40 24.68 kN/m 80% of 3 floors imposed load = 3 × 5.4 × 0.8 = 12.96 kN/m	24.68	69.36	12.96
3rd floor: *dead wt.:* Floor: 4.8 × 3 × 1.2* = 17.28 Wall: 7.40 24.68 kN/m 70% of 4 floors imposed load = 4 × 5.4 × 0.7 = 15.12 kN/m	24.68	94.04	15.12
2nd floor: *dead wt.:* Floor: 4.8 × 3 × 1.2* = 17.28 Wall: 7.40 24.68 kN/m 60% of 5 floors imposed load = 5 × 5.4 × 0.6 = 16.2 kN/m	24.68	118.72	16.2
1st floor: *dead wt:* Floor: 4.8 × 3 × 1.2* = 17.28 Wall: 7.40 24.68 kN/m 60% of 6 floors imposed load = 6 × 5.4 × 0.6 = 19.44 kN/m	24.68	143.40	19.44
Ground floor: *dead wt.:* Floor: 4.8 × 3 × 1.2* = 17.28 Wall: 7.40 24.68 kN/m 60% of 7 floors imposed load = 7 × 5.4 × 0.6 = 22.68 kN/m	24.68	168.08	22.68

* The factor 1.2 comes from Table 4 CP110:Part 1:1972.

10.4.1 Inner Leaf

Table 10.2 Loading on Wall B/m just above floor. Inner Leaf

Floor level considered		Load/m run		
		Dead at floor	Cumulative dead to floor G_k	Cumulative imposed to floor Q_k
6th floor Roof dead wt. $-$ $3.5 \times 3 \times 0.45^{+}$ Wall (roof to 6th floor) 2.42×2.85	$= 4.725$ $= \underline{6.897}$ 11.62kN/m	11.62	11.62	2.025
5th floor Floor dead wt. $-$ $4.8 \times 3 \times 0.45$ Wall 6th to 5th *90% imposed load$-$ $2 \times 2.025 \times .90$	$= 6.48$ $= \underline{6.897}$ 13.38 $= 3.645 \text{ kN/m}$	13.38	25.0	3.645
4th floor Dead wt. same as 5th *80% of three floors imposed load $3 \times 2.025 \times .8$	 $= 4.86 \text{ kN/m}$	13.38	38.38	4.86
3rd floor Dead wt. same as 5th *70% of 4 floors imposed load $4 \times 2.025 \times .7$	 $=$ $= 5.67 \text{ kN/m}$	13.38	51.76	5.67
2nd floor Dead wt. same as 5th *60% of 5 floors imposed load$=$ $5 \times 2.025 \times .6$	 $= 6.08 \text{ kN/m}$	13.38	65.14	6.08
1st floor Dead wt. same as 5th *60% of 6 floors imposed load $=$ $6 \times 2.025 \times .6$	 $= 7.29 \text{ kN/m}$	13.38	78.54	7.29
Ground floor Dead wt. same as 5th *60% of 7 floors imposed load $=$ $7 \times 2.025 \times .6$	 $= 8.51 \text{ kN/m}$	13.38	91.90	8.51

+ 0.45 from Table 4 CP 110: Part 1: 1972
* Imposed load reduction from Table 2 CP 3: Chapter V: Part 1

10.4.2 Outer leaf
Load/m at floor: $24.2 \times 3 = 72.6$ kN/m
Imposed load — Nil

10.4.3 Total dead weight of the building above G.L.
(neglecting openings etc.)
G_k $= 3.5 \times 21 \times 10.5 + 6 \times 4.8 \times 21 \times 10.5 + (12 \times 2.6 \times 4.25 \times 2.85 + 4 \times$ $2 \times 2.42 \times 4.25 \times 2.85 + 2 \times 21 \times 2.6 \times 4.25 \times 2.85 + 21 \times 2 \times 2 \times$ $2.42 \times 4.25 \times 2.85) \times 7 = 37903.4$ kN.

10.5 WIND LOADING

10.5.1 General Stability
To explain the method, only walls A and B are considered in the calculation, hence wind blowing from either north or south direction is critical and evaluated. In the east-west direction the cavity and corridor walls will provide the resistance to wind loading. In an actual design, the designer must of course check that the structure is safe for wind blowing east–west and vice-versa.

In the calculation below it has further been assumed that the walls act as independent cantilevers: and hence moments or forces are apportioned according to their stiffness.

10.5.2 Wind Loads (CP 3 Chapter V: Part 2)

$V_s = V \times S_1 \times S_2 \times S_3$
Factor S_1 and $S_3 = 1.0$

Using ground roughness category 3, Class B
Ht. of the building = 21.0 m
From Table 3 CP 3 Chapter V: Part 2 $S_2 = 0.91$

Therefore design wind speed
$V_s = 50 \times 1 \times 1 \times 0.91 = 45.5$ m/s

and dynamic wind pressure
$q = 0.613 \times (45.5)^2 = 1269.0$ N/m^2

From Clause 7.3 CP3 Chapter V: Part 2
Total wind force $F = C_f . q A_e$ ($C_f = 1.1$ Table 10)
A_e = effective surface area

Total Max. B. M. $= F \times h/2$ where h is the height under consideration.

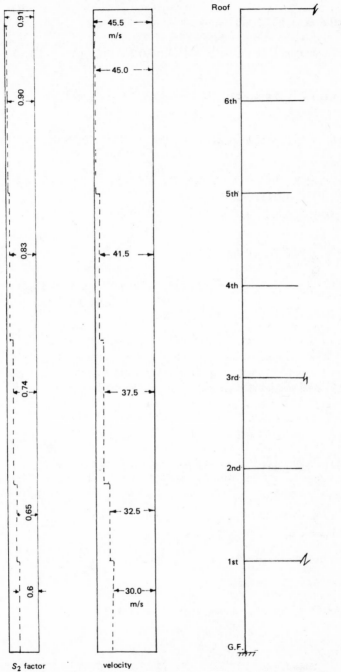

Fig. 10.3 — Showing the variation of the factor S_2 and the wind velocity along the height of the building. (Assumptions made in the design shown in full lines).

Total B.M. just above floor level

6th floor: $C_f q A_e \times h/2 = 1.1 \times (1269/10^3) \times 21 \times 3 \times \dfrac{3}{2} = 131.9$ kNm

5th floor: $1.1 \times (1269/10^3) \times 21 \times 6 \times 3 = 527.6$ kNm

4th floor: $(1.1 \times 1269 \times 21/10^3) \times 9 \times \dfrac{9}{2} = 1187.20$ kNm

3rd floor: $29.313 \times (12 \times 12/2) = 2110.54$ kNm

2nd floor: $29.313 \times (15 \times 15/2) = 3297.70$ kNm

1st floor: $29.313 \times (18 \times 18/2) = 4748.71$ kNm

Ground floor: $1.1 \times (1269/10^3) \times 21 \times 21 \times \dfrac{21}{2} = 6463.72$ kNm.

In the calculation the factor S_2 has been kept constant (Fig. 10.3), which means the design will be a bit conservative. However, the reader can vary the S_2 factor as given in the Fig. 10.3 taken from Table 3 (CP 3) which means the wind speed will be variable depending on the height of the building.

10.5.3 Assumed section of wall resisting the wind moment
The flange which acts together with the web of I-section is the lesser of the three,

i)   12 times thickness of flange + thickness of web

ii)   Centre line to Centre line of walls

iii) $\frac{1}{3}$ of span.

Wall A   Calculation of second moment of area

Wind direction ———➤   1.34 m

|◄——— 4.25 m ———►|

Neglecting the outer skin of cavity-wall flange:

$$I_A = 2 \times \frac{(0.125)^3 \times 1.34}{12} + 0.1025 \times 1.34 \times (2.07)^2 + \frac{(4.045)^3 \times 0.1025}{12}$$

$$= 1.169 + 0.565 = 1.734 \text{ m}^4$$

Wall B. The flange width which acts with channel section has been assumed as half of the I-section.

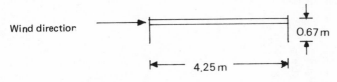

Neglecting the outer skin of the cavity-wall flange:

$$I_B = 2 \times (0.67 \times \frac{(0.1025)^3}{12} + 0.1025 \times 0.67 \times (2.07)^2) + 2 \times 0.1025 \times \frac{(4.045)^3}{12}$$

$$= 0.571 + 1.13 = 1.7 \text{m}^4 \quad .$$

Total second moment of area $\Sigma I = 12 I_A + 4 I_B$

for the building $\qquad = 12 \times 1.734 + 4 \times 1.7 = 27.61 \text{m}^4 \quad .$

Moment carried by Wall A, $M_A = Total\ Moment \times I_A/\Sigma I = \dfrac{1.734}{27.61} \times M$

$$= 0.06266 M \quad .$$

Moment carried by Wall B, $M_B = 1.7/27.61\ M$

$$= 0.0616 M$$

Table 10.3: Distribution of bending moment stresses and shear force in walls

Just above floor level	WALL A		WALL B	
	Bending stress N/mm²	Shear force kN	Bending stress N/mm²	Shear force kN
6th floor:				
Wall A $= \dfrac{M_A Y}{I_A} = \dfrac{0.06266 \times 131.9^*}{1.734} \times \dfrac{2.125}{10^3}$	±0.01	5.5	±0.01	5.41
Wall B $= \dfrac{M_B Y}{I_B} = \dfrac{0.0616 \times 131.9^*}{1.7 \times 10^3} \times 2.125$				
5th floor:				
Wall A $= \dfrac{0.06266 \times 527.6^* \times 21.25}{1.734 \times 10^3}$	±0.04	11.0	±0.04	10.83
Wall B $= \dfrac{0.0616 \times 527.6^* \times 2.125}{1.7 \times 10^3}$				
4th floor:				
Wall A $= \dfrac{0.06266 \times 2.125}{1.734 \times 10^3} \times 1187.2^*$		16.5		16.24

Wall B = $\dfrac{0.0616 \times 2.125}{1.7 \times 10^3} \times 1187.2^*$

= 0.000077×1187.2

3rd floor:
Wall A = $0.768 \times 10^{-4} \times 2110.54^*$ ±0.162 22.0 ±0.163 21.65
Wall B = $0.77 \times 10^{-4} \times 2110.54^*$

2nd floor:
Wall A = $0.768 \times 10^{-4} \times 3297.7^*$ ±0.253 27.5 ±0.254 27.06
Wall B = $0.77 \times 10^{-4} \times 3297.7^*$

1st floor:
Wall A = $0.768 \times 10^{-4} \times 4748.71^*$ ±0.365 33.0 ±0.366 32.5
Wall B = $0.77 \times 10^{-4} \times 4748.71^*$

Ground floor:
Wall A = $0.768 \times 10^{-4} \times 6463.72^*$ ±0.496 38.50 ±0.498 37.9
Wall B = $0.77 \times 10^{-4} \times 6463.72^*$

* From Section 10.5.2

10.6 DESIGN LOADS:

10.6.1 Load Combination for Ultimate Limits State: Clause 22 BS 5628

Wall A

6th Floor:

i) Dead and imposed load $= 1.4\,G_K + 1.6\,Q_K$

$$= 1.4 \times 20 + 1.6 \times 5.4 = 28 + 8.64$$

$$= 36.64 \text{ kN/m}$$

Stress $= (36.64 \times 10^3)/(102.5 \times 10^3) = 0.357 \text{ N/mm}^2$.

ii) Dead + wind $= 0.9\,G_K + 1.4\,W_K$

a) Stress $= (0.9 \times 28 \times 10^3)/(1.4 \times 102.5 \times 10^3) - 1.4 \times 0.01$

$$= 0.176 - 0.014 = +0.162 \text{ N/mm}^2 \quad .$$

No tension develops, hence safe.

Leeward side

b) Dead + wind $= 1.4\,G_K + 1.4\,W_K$

$$= (28 \times 10^3)/(102.5 \times 10^3) + 0.014 \text{ (from above)}$$

$$= 0.273 + 0.014 = 0.287 \text{ N/mm}^2 \quad .$$

iii) Dead + live + wind $= 1.2\,G_K + 1.2\,Q_K + 1.2\,W_K$

Stress $= (0.273 \times 1.2)/1.4 + (8.64 \times 1.2)/(1.6 \times 102.5) \pm 1.2 \times 0.01$

$$= 0.234 + 0.0632 \pm 0.012 = 0.31 \text{ or } 0.285 \text{ N/mm}^2 \; .$$

No tension developing, hence safe.

The load combination which produces severe condition is:

Design + imposed $= 1.4\,G_K + 1.6\,Q_K$.

Therefore, the design load $= 36.64 \text{ kN/m}$.

5th Floor:
i)   Dead and imposed $= 1.4\,G_K + 1.6\,Q_K$

$= 1.4 \times 44.68 + 1.6 \times 9.72$

$= 62.55 + 15.55 = 78.10 \text{ kN/m}$

Stress $= (78.10 \times 10^3)/(102.5 \times 10^3) = 0.76 \text{ N/mm}^2$.

ii) Dead + wind $= 0.9\,G_K + 1.4\,W_K$

a)   Stress $= (0.9 \times 62.55 \times 10^3)/(1.4 \times 102.5 \times 1000)$
$- 1.4 \times 0.04$

$= 0.39 - 0.056 = 0.334 \text{ N/mm}^2$.

No tension develops, hence safe.

Leeward side
b)   Dead + wind $= 1.4\,G_K + 1.4\,W_K$

Stress $= (62.55 \times 10^3)/(102.5 \times 10^3) + 0.056$

$= 0.61 + 0.056 = 0.67 \text{ N/mm}^2$.

iii) Dead + live + wind $= 1.2\,G_K + 1.2\,Q_K + 1.2\,W_K$

Stress $= (0.61 \times 1.2)/1.4 + (15.55 \times 1.2)/(1.6 \times 102.5)$
$\pm 1.2 \times 0.04$

$= 0.52 + 0.11 \pm 0.048$

$= 0.68 \text{ or } 0.58 \text{ N/mm}^2$.

No tension developing, hence safe.
Hence the load combination which produces the severe condition is case (i)
and the load is 78.10 kN/m   .

4th Floor:
i)   Dead + imposed $= 1.4\,G_K + 1.6\,Q_K$

$= 1.4 \times 69.36 + 1.6 \times 12.96$

$= 97.10 + 20.74 \text{ kN/m}$

Stress $= (97.10 \times 10^3)/(102.5 \times 10^3)$
$+ (20.74 \times 10^3)/(102.5 \times 10^3)$

$= 0.95 + 0.20 = 1.15 \text{ N/mm}^2$.

ii) Dead + wind $= 0.9\,G_K + 1.4\,W_K$.

a) Stress $= (0.95 \times 0.9)/1.4 - 1.4 \times 0.09$.

$= 0.61 - 0.126 = 0.484 \text{ N/mm}^2$ (No tension).

Leeward Side
b) Dead + wind $= 1.4\,G_K + 1.4\,W_K$

Stress $= 0.95 + 0.126 = 1.08 \text{ N/mm}^2$

iii) Dead + imposed + wind $= 1.2\,G_K + 1.2\,Q_K + 1.2\,W_K$.

Stress $= (0.95 \times 1.2)/1.4 + (1.2 \times .20)/1.6 \pm 1.2 \times 0.09$

$= 0.814 + 0.15 \pm 0.108$

$= 1.07$ or 0.856 N/mm^2 (No tension) .

In this case also the severe loading condition appears to be case (i).

3rd Floor:
i) Design + imposed load $= 1.4\,G_K + 1.6\,Q_K$

$= 1.4 \times 94.04 + 1.6 \times 15.12$

$= 131.66 + 24.19 = 155.85 \text{ kN/m}$

Stress $= (131.66 \times 10^3)/(102.5 \times 10^3)$
$+ (24.19 \times 10^3)/(102.5 \times 10^3)$

$= 1.28 + 0.24 = 1.52 \text{ N/mm}^2$.

ii) Dead + wind $= 0.9\,G_K + 1.4\,W_K$

a) $= (0.9 \times 1.28)/1.4 = 1.4 \times 0.162$

$= 0.823 - 0.227 = 0.596 \text{ N/mm}^2$ (No tension) .

Leeward
b)   Dead + wind $= 1.4\,G_K + 1.4\,W_K$

$= 1.28 + 0.227 = 1.51\ \text{N/mm}^2$.

iii) Dead + live + wind $= 1.2\,G_K + 1.2\,Q_K + 1.2\,W_K$

$= (1.28 \times 1.2)/1.4 + (0.24 \times 1.2)/1.6 \pm 1.2 \times 0.162$

$= 1.097 + 0.18 \pm 0.194$

$= 1.47\ \text{N/mm}^2$ or $1.08\ \text{N/mm}^2$ (No tension develops).

The critical load combination is case (i) and the load is 155.85 kN/m .

2nd Floor:
i)   Design + imposed load $= 1.4\,G_K + 1.6\,Q_K$

$= 1.4 \times 118.72 + 1.6 \times 16.2$

$= 166.2 + 25.9 = 192.10\ \text{kN/m}$.

    Stress $= (1.4 \times 118.72 \times 10^3)/(102.5 \times 10^3)$
$+ (1.6 \times 16.2 \times 10^3)/(102.5 \times 10^3)$

$= 1.62 + 0.25 = 1.87\ \text{N/mm}^2$.

ii) Dead + wind $= 0.9\,G_K + 1.4\,W_K$.

a)   Stress $= (0.9 \times 1.62)/1.4 - (1.4 \times 0.253)$

$= 1.04 - 0.35 = 0.69\ \text{N/mm}^2$ (No tension) .

Leeward
b)   Dead + wind $= 1.4\,G_K + 1.4\,W_K$

    Stress $= 1.62 + 1.4 \times 0.253 = 1.97\ \text{N/mm}^2$.

iii) Dead + imposed + wind $= 1.2\,G_K + 1.2\,Q_K + 1.2\,W_K$

$= (1.62 \times 1.2)/1.4 + (0.25 \times 1.2)/1.6 \pm 1.2 \times 0.253$

$= 1.39 + 0.19 \pm 0.30$

$= 1.88$ or $1.28\ \text{N/mm}^2$ (No tension) .

The critical load combination which produces severe condition is:

Dead + wind = $1.4\,G_K + 1.4\,Q_K$ and the design load therefore is

$$= (1.97 \times 102.5 \times 10^3)/10^3 = 202\ \text{kN/m}\quad.$$

1st Floor:

i) Dead + imposed $= 1.4\,G_K + 1.6\,Q_K$

$= 1.4 \times 143.40 + 1.6 \times 19.44$

$= 200.76 + 31.10 = 231.86\ \text{kN/m}\quad.$

Stress $= (200.76 \times 10^3)/(102.5 \times 10^3)$
$(31.10 \times 10^3)/(102.5 \times 10^3)$

$= 1.96 + 0.30 = 2.26\ \text{N/mm}^2\quad.$

ii) Dead + wind $= 0.9\,G_K + 1.4\,W_K$

a) Stress $= (1.96 \times 0.9)/1.4 - 1.4 \times 0.365$

$= 1.26 - 0.51 = 0.75\ \text{N/mm}^2\,(\text{No tension})\quad.$

Leeward

b) Dead + wind $= 1.4\,G_K + 1.4\,W_K\quad.$

Stress $= 1.96 + 0.51 = 2.47\ \text{N/mm}^2\quad.$

iii) Dead + imposed + wind $= 1.2\,G_K + 1.2\,Q_K + 1.2\,W_K\quad.$

Stress $= (1.2 \times 1.96)/1.4 + (1.2 \times 0.3)/1.6$
$\pm (1.2 \times 0.51)/1.4$

$= 1.68 + 0.225 \pm 0.437$

$= 2.34\ \text{or}\ 1.47\ \text{N/mm}^2\,(\text{No tension develops})\quad.$

The design load for this floor is equal to:

$$= (2.47 \times 102.5 \times 10^3)/10^3 = 253.18\ \text{kN/m}\quad.$$

Ground Floor:
i)   Dead + imposed $= 1.4\,G_K + 1.6\,Q_K$.

Stress $= (1.4 \times 168.08)/102.5 + (1.6 \times 22.68)/102.5$

$= 2.3 + 0.354 = 2.654 \text{ N/mm}^2$.

ii) Dead + wind $= 0.9\,G_K + 1.4\,W_K$.

a)   Stress $= (2.3 \times .9)/1.4 - 1.4 \times 0.496$

$= 1.48 - 0.69 = 0.78 \text{ N/mm}^2 \text{ (No tension)}$.

Leeward
b)   Dead + wind $= 1.4\,G_K + 1.4\,W_K$

Stress $= 2.3 + 0.69 \approx 2.99 \text{ N/mm}^2$.

iii) Dead + imposed + wind $= 1.2\,G_K + 1.2\,Q_K + 1.2\,W_K$

$= (2.3 \times 1.2)/1.4 + (1.2 \times .354)/1.6$
$\pm 1.2 \times 0.496$

$= 1.97 + 0.266 \pm 0.595$

$= 2.83 \text{ or } 1.64 \text{ N/mm}^2 \text{ (No tension develops)}$.

The load combination, dead + wind $= 1.4\,G_K + 1.4\,W_K$ produces the severe condition and hence the design load is equal to

$(2.99 \times 102.5 \times 10^3)/10^3 = 306.48 \text{ kN/m}$.

Note: From section 10.5.2 the total wind force $F = C_f.q.A_c$

$= (1.1 \times 1269)/10^3 \times 21 \times 21$

$= 615.6 \text{ kN}$.

$615.6 \times \gamma_f > 0.015\,G_K \text{ } (G_K \text{ from section 10.4.3})$

or $615.6 \times 1.4 = 861.84 \text{ kN} > 0.015 \times 37903.4 = 568.6 \text{ kN,}$

hence in the load combination $0.015\,G_K$ has not been considered. This is true for all other floors also.

10.6.1.1 *Selection of brick and mortar combinations for Wall A: BS 5628*
Design vertical load resistance of wall = $(\beta t f_k)/\gamma_m$ Clause 32.2.1

Eccentricity $e = 0$, S.R. $= \frac{3}{4} \times (2.85 \times 10^3)/102.5 = 20.85$,

hence $\beta = 0.67$ (Table 7), $\gamma_m = 3.5$ (see section 10.3.1)

Table 10.4 Design Load and Characteristic Brickwork Strength

Floor	Design load/m (Section 10.6.1)	Design Characteristic Strength $= \dfrac{\text{Design load} \times \gamma_m}{\beta t}$ f_k (N/mm^2)	f_k from Table 2 and Clause 23.1.2 N/mm^2
6th	36.64	1.87	20 N/mm^2 brick in 1:1:6 mortar $f_k = 1.15 \times 5.8 = 6.67$N/mm^2
5th	78.10	3.98	20 N/mm^2 brick in 1:1:6 mortar $f_k = 1.15 \times 5.8 = 6.67$N/mm^2
4th	117.84	6.0	20 N/mm^2 brick in 1:1:6 mortar $f_k = 1.15 \times 5.8 = 6.67$N/mm^2
3rd	155.85	7.94	20 N/mm^2 brick in 1:$\frac{1}{4}$:3 mortar $f_k = 8.51$ N/mm^2
2nd	202.0	10.29	35 N/mm^2 brick in 1:$\frac{1}{4}$:3 mortar $f_k = 1.15 \times 11.4 = 13.11$N/mm^2
1st	253.18	12.9	35 N/mm^2 brick in 1:$\frac{1}{4}$:3 mortar $f_k = 1.15 \times 11.4 = 13.11$N/mm^2
G.F.	306.48	15.62	50 N/mm^2 brick in 1:$\frac{1}{4}$:3 mortar $f_k = 1.15 \times 15 = 17.25$N/mm^2

Check for Shear Stress:

Design characteristic shear $f_v = \gamma_f \, \gamma_{mv} \dfrac{\text{shear force}}{\text{area}} < 0.35 + 0.6 \, g_A$ (Clause 25)

$\gamma_f = 1.4$ and $\gamma_{mv} = 2.5$ (10.3.1). The value of shear force is taken from Table 10.3.

6th Floor
Design characteristic shear stress:

$$\frac{1.4 \times 2.5 \times 5.5 \times 10^3}{102.5 \times 4250} = 0.044 \text{ N/mm}^2 < 0.35 + \frac{0.6 \times 20 \times 0.9 \times 10^3}{102.5 \times 1000}$$

$$= 0.45 \text{ (safe)} \quad.$$

Ground Floor
Design characteristic shear stress:

$$\frac{1.4 \times 2.5 \times 38.5 \times 10^3}{102.5 \times 4250} = 0.31 \text{ N/mm}^2 < 0.35 + \frac{0.6 \times 168.08 \times 0.9 \times 10^3}{102.5 \times 1000}$$

$$= 1.23 \text{ N/mm}^2 \quad.$$

There is no need to check at any other level, since shear is not a problem for this type of structure.

The BS 5628 recommends g_A as the design vertical load per unit area of wall cross-section due to vertical load calculated from the appropriate loading condition specified in Clause 22. The critical condition of shear will be with no imposed load just after and during the construction.

10.6.2 Load Combinations: Wall B
The design principle has been covered in great detail for Wall A, hence for Wall B this will be limited to the ground floor level to explain further salient points.

Inner-leaf Wall B – Ground Floor Level:
i)   Dead + imposed load $= 1.4 \, G_K + 1.6 \, Q_K$ (G_K and Q_K from Table 10.2)

   Stress $= (1.4 \times 91.9 \times 10^3)/(102.5 \times 10^3)$
                              $+ (1.6 \times 8.51 \times 10^3)/(102.5 \times 10^3)$

                             $= 1.26 + 0.13 = 1.39 \text{ N/mm}^2 \quad.$

ii) Dead + imposed

a) Windward side: $0.9\,G_K + 1.4\,W_K$.

Stress $= (0.9 \times 1.26)/1.4 - 1.4 \times 0.498$

$= 0.81 - 0.70 = 0.11 \text{ N/mm}^2$
(No tension develops)   .

b) Leeward side: $1.4\,G_K + 1.4\,W_K$

Stress $= 1.26 + 1.4 \times 0.498 = 1.96 \text{ N/mm}^2$.

iii) Dead + imposed + wind $= 1.2\,G_K + 1.2\,Q_K + 1.2\,W_K$

Stress $= (1.26 \times 1.2)/1.4 + (0.13 \times 1.2)/1.6 \pm 1.2 \times 0.498$

$= 1.08 + 0.098 \pm 0.98$

$= 1.78 \text{ or } 0.58 \text{ N/mm}^2$ (No tension develops)   .

The worst combination for this wall just above ground level also is

dead + wind, and the design load
$= (1.96 \times 102.5 \times 10^3)/10^3 = 201 \text{ kN/m}$.

10.6.2.1 Selection of Brick and Mortar for Innerleaf of Wall B
The design vertical load resistance of wall is $\beta t\, f_k/\gamma_m$ Clause 32.2.1

The value of β depends on the eccentricity of loading, hence the value of e needs to be evaluated before design can be completed.

10.6.2.2 Calculation of Eccentricity
The worst combination of loading for obtaining the value of e at top of the wall is shown in Fig. 10.4.

Axial Load $P = (0.9 \times 78.54 + 1.6 \times 7.29)$ (G_K and Q_K from Table 10.2)

$= (70.69 + 11.66) = 82.35 \text{ kN/m}$.

1st floor Load $P_1 = (1.4 \times 6.48 + 1.6 \times 2.025)$ (see Table 10.2)

$= 12.31 \text{ kN/m}$.

$$e = \frac{P_1 t}{6(P + P_1)} = \frac{12.31t}{6(82.35 + 12.31)} = 0.0217\,t = 2.22 \text{ mm}$$

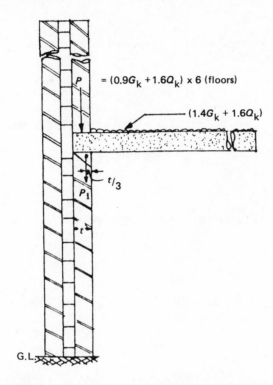

Fig. 10.4 – Load combination for calculating the eccentricity.

Wind Blowing N.S. Direction (Case 1):
A part of the panel B will be subjected to suction, if the wind is blowing in N-S direction.

$$V_s = V.S_1.S_2'.S_3{}^* = 50 \times 1 \times 1 \times 0.64 \text{ (ground roughness category}$$
$$\text{A, CP3 Chapter V Part 2)}$$
$$= 32 \text{ m/s}$$

$$q = 0.613 \times (32)^2 = 627.8 \text{ N/mm}^2$$

B.M. at centre of the panel $= 627.8 \times (C_p e + Cp_i)h^2 \times 0.104$

(B.M. coefficient for 4 sided simply supported panel is 0.104)

$$= 627.8 \times (1.1 + 0.2) \times (2.85)^2 \times 0.104$$

$$= 689.4 \text{ Nm/m} \quad (Cp_e \text{ and } Cp_i - \text{CP3 Chapter V: Part 2})$$

Note: *The localised effect is considered here, hence S_2 for Category A is being used.

B.M./leaf = 689.4/2   = 344.7 Nm/m (Since both leaves are of same stiffness)

e_{centre} = (344.7 × 10³)/
         (94.66 × 10³)   = 3.64 mm

where $P + P_1$ = 94.66 kN/m

Resultant e_{cc} = (2.22/2) + 3.64 = 4.75 mm = 0.0463t .

Wind Blowing West–East Direction (Case 2):
The panel B is not only subjected to dead and imposed loads, but also subjected to wind loading from west to east direction.

The B.M. at the centre   = 0.104 × $q\,h^2$ (q from section 10.5.2)

                = 0.104 × 1.4 × 1269 × 1.1 × (2.85)² (Considering the loading from overall stability)

                = 1650.84 Nm/m   .

B.M. /leaf as above   = 1650.84/2 = 825.42 Nm/m   .

e_{cc} at the centre   = (825.42 × 10³)/(94.66 × 10³) = 8.72 mm   .

Therefore resultant e = 8.72 − (2.22/2) (The bending moment induced due to wind loading acts against those being due to the vertical load)

                = 7.61 mm = 0.074t .

Since resultant eccentricity for Case 2 is greater than Case 1, Case 2 eccentricity is considered in the design.

Calculation of Characteristic Compressive Stress f_k for Wall B (Inner leaf)

Design load $\qquad\qquad = \dfrac{\beta t f_k}{\gamma_m}$ Clause 32.2.1 BS 5628

Slenderness ratio $\qquad = (\frac{3}{4} \times 2.85 \times 10^3)/(\frac{2}{3}(102.5 + 102.5))$

$\qquad\qquad\qquad\qquad = 15.6$ and $e_R = 0.074t$, therefore

β (from Table 7) $\qquad = 0.81$ from linear interpolation, therefore

$0.81 \times 102.5 f_k \qquad = 3.5 \times 201$

$f_k \qquad\qquad\qquad = 8.47$ N/mm^2 .

Use 20 N/mm^2 brick in $1:\frac{1}{4}:3$ mortar; $f_k = 7.4 \times 1.15$

$\qquad\qquad\qquad\qquad = 8.51$ N/mm$^2 > 8.47$ N/mm^2 (Safe) .

Check for Shear

Design characteristic shear stress $= \gamma_{mv} \times \dfrac{\text{shear force}}{\text{area}}$

$$= \frac{2.5 \times 37.9 \times 10^3}{2 \times 102.5 \times 4250} = 0.108 \text{ N/mm}^2$$

$$< 0.35 + \frac{0.9 \times 91.90 \times 10^3}{1000 \times 102.5}$$

$$= 1.16 \text{ N/mm}^2 \text{ (Safe)} .$$

10.6.2.3 *Design of the outer leaf of the cavity wall B in G.F.*

Load Combination

a) Windward side: dead + imposed = $0.9 \, G_K + 1.2 \, W_K$ (300 mm projection of roof

Note: $\gamma_f = 1.2$ is used as per Clause 22.

Stress $\quad = \dfrac{0.9(7 \times 7.26 + .30 \times 3.5) \times 10^3}{102.5 \times 1000} - 1.2 \times 0.498$

$$= 0.455 - 0.598 = -0.14 \text{ N/mm}^2 \quad .$$

b) Leeward Side: dead + imposed $= 1.4\,G_K + 1.2\,W_K$

   Stress $\quad = 1.4 \times 0.455 + 0.598 = 1.23 \text{ N/mm}^2 \quad .$

The design is similar to the inner leaf and will not be considered any further. The slight tension which is developing is of no consequence, since 6 to 10% of the dead and imposed load will be transferred to the outer leaf even in case where slab is supported on the inner skin. The bending stress caused by the wind will be smaller if S_2 factor is assumed variable as explained in section 10.5.2. The staircase and lift well will also provide the stability against the wind which has been neglected. However, any facing brick having water absorption between 7 to 12% in $1:\frac{1}{4}:3$ mortar may be used, provided that it satisfies the lateral load design. The grade of mortar is kept the same as for the inner leaf.

Characteristic flexural strength

$$f_{kx} \quad = 0.14 \times 3.5 \qquad\qquad (\gamma_m = 3.5)$$

$$0.49 \text{ N/mm}^2 < 0.5 \text{ N/mm}^3 \qquad \text{(Table 3)} \quad .$$

Design characteristic shear as in inner leaf

$$0.108 \; < 0.35 \; \frac{0.9 \times (7 \times 7.26 \times .3 \times 3.5) \times 10^3}{102.5 \times 10^3}$$

$$= 0.80 \text{ N/mm}^2 \quad \text{(Safe)} \quad .$$

Instead of the conventional design calculations described in this chapter a more sophisticated analysis of the structure is possible by idealising it as a frame with vertical loading as shown in Fig. 10.5. Similarly, the structure can be idealised and replaced by a two-dimensional frame (Fig. 10.6) and analysed as discussed in Chapter 6 for wind loading.

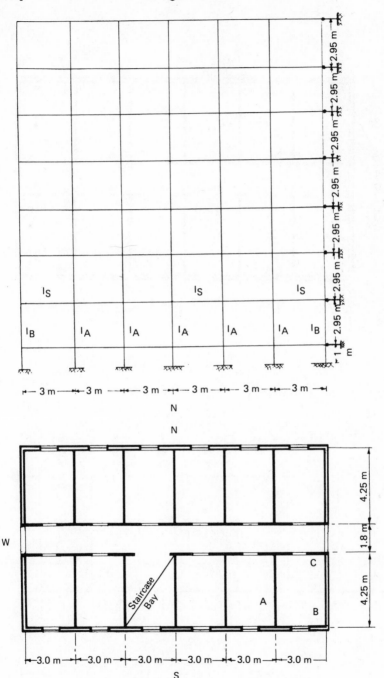

Fig. 10.5 – Idealised structure for vertical load design.

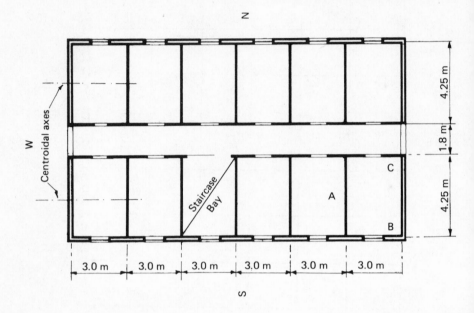

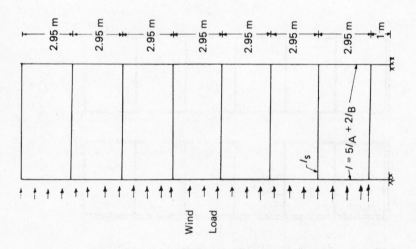

Fig. 10.6 – Idealised structure for wind load design.

10.7 DESIGN OF PANEL FOR LATERAL LOADING: BS 5628 (Limit State)

To explain the principle of the design only panel B between 6th floor and roof will be considered. The low precompression on the inner leaf is ignored in this design.

Assume: Inner leaf 102.5 mm brickwork in 1:1:6 mortar
Outer leaf 102.5 mm brickwork with facing brick in 1:1:6 mortar
Boundary conditions: Two sides simply supported and two sides fixed as shown in Fig. 10.7.

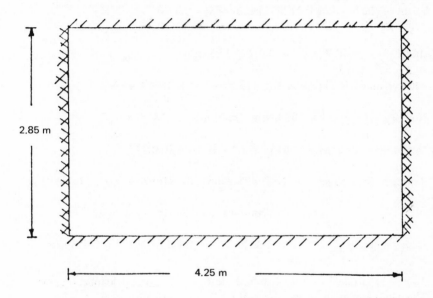

Fig. 10.7 – Panel, simply supported top and bottom and fixed at its vertical edges.

10.7.1 Limiting Dimension: Clause 36.3 BS 5628: Case B

The dimensions $h \times l$ of panels supported on four edges should be equal to or less than $2250 \, t_{ef}^2$

Area = $2.85 \times 4.25 = 12.12 \text{m}^2$: $t_e = \frac{2}{3} \times 205 = 137$ mm

$2025 \times (137)^2/10^6 = 38 \text{ m}^2 > 12.12 \text{ m}^2$ (satisfactory)

$50 \times t_e = 6.85 > 4.25$ (satisfactory) .

10.7.2 Characteristic Wind Load W_K

The corner panel is subjected to local wind suctions. From CP 3: Chapter V, total coefficient of wind pressure,

$$Cp - Cp_1 = -1.1 - (+0.2) = (-)\,1.3 \quad .$$

The design wind velocity: $V_S = V \times S_1 \times S_2 \times S_3$,

where S_1 and $S_3 = 1$

Using ground roughness Category (3), Class A
height of the building = 21 m, Therefore $S_3 = 0.956$.

therefore $V_S = 50 \times 1 \times 1 \times 0.956 = 47.8$ m/s

and dynamic wind pressure = $(0.613 \times (47.8)^2)/10^3 = 1.4$ kN/m^2 .

Now $W_K = 1.4 \times 1.3 = 1.82$ kN/m^2 (suction)   .

Design moment in panel $= \alpha W_K \; \gamma_f \, L^2$ (Clause 36.4.1)

Aspect ratio of panel $= 2.85/4.25 = 0.67$, therefore $\alpha = 0.032$ (Table 9)

Assuming $\mu = 0.30$ from (Table 9)

Design moment $= 0.032 \times 1.82 \times 1.4 \times (4.25)^2 = 1.47$ kNm/m   .

Note: γ_f is taken as 1.4 since inner leaf is an important loadbearing element. The designer may, however, use $\gamma_f = 1.2$ in other circumstances.

Design moment/leaf = $1.47/2 = 0.736$ kNm/m (Since both leaves are of equal stiffness)

Design moment of resistance $= f_{kx}\, Z/\gamma_m$ where $\gamma_m = 3.5$

$$= f_{kx} \cdot 1000 \times 102.5^2)/(6 \times 3.5)$$

$$= 500298\, f_{kx}\ \text{mm}^3/\text{m} \quad .$$

Therefore $f_{kx} = (0.736 \times 10^6)/(500298) = 1.47$ N/mm$^2 < 1.5$ N/mm^2 .

Use bricks having water absorption less than 7% in 1:1:6 mortar.

10.8 DESIGN FOR ACCIDENTAL DAMAGE

10.8.1 Introduction

The building which has been designed earlier in this chapter falls in Category 2 (Table 12 BS 5628) hence the additional recommendation of Clause 37 to limit the extent of accidental damage must be met over and above the recommendations in Clause 20.2 for the preservation of structural integrity.

Three options are given in the Code in Table 12. Before these options are discussed it would be proper to consider whether the walls A and B in the ground floor, carrying heaviest precompression, can be designated as protected elements.

10.8.2 Protected Wall

A protected wall must be capable of resisting 34 kN/m^2 from any direction. Let us examine wall A first.

Wall A

Load combination: $0.95\,G_K + 0.35\,Q_K + 0.35\,W_K$ (Clause 22)

$$G_K = \text{the load just below the first floor} \quad .$$

Axial Stress $= \dfrac{10^3[0.95 \times (168.08 - 7.4) + 0.35 \times 22.68]}{102.5 \times 1000}$

$\pm\, 0.35 \times 0.365$ (See Table 10.1 and 10.3)

$= 1.57 \pm 0.1277$

$= 1.442 \text{ or } 1.70 \text{ kN/mm}^2 \quad .$

Therefore $n = (1.442 \times 102.5 \times 1000)/1000 = 147.8 \text{ kN/m} \quad .$

Lateral Strength of Wall with Two Returns:

q_{lat} $= k.8tn/h^2\,\gamma_m$ (Clause 36.8 and Table 10)

l/h $= 4.25/2.85 = 1.49, \quad \text{hence } k = 2.265$

q_{lat} $= (2.265 \times 8 \times 102.5 \times 147.8)/(2.85)^2 \times 1.05)$

$= 33.8 \text{ kN/m}^2 < 34 \text{ kN/m}^2 \quad .$

hence this wall cannot strictly be classified as a protected member.

Since wall A, carrying a higher precompression, just fails to resist 34 kN/m^2 pressure, wall B with a lower precompression obviously would not meet the requirement for a protected member.

Further, for both walls

$$h_{/t} = \frac{(2.85 \times 10^3)}{102.5} = 27.8 > 25$$

Neither wall A or B can resist 34 kN/m^2. Even if they did, they do not fulfil the requirement of clause 36.8 that

$$h_{/t} \leqslant 25 \quad .$$

It may be commented that the basis of this provision in the code is obscure and conflicts with the results of tests on laterally loaded walls. Other options therefore need to be considered in designing against accidental damage.

10.8.3 Accidental damage: options
Option 1: Option 1 requires the designer to establish that all vertical and horizontal elements are removable one at a time without leading to collapse of any significant portion of the structure. So far as the horizontal members are concerned, this option is superfluous if concrete floor or roof slabs are used, since their structural design must conform to the clause 3.1.2.2 of CP 110:1972.

Option 3: For the horizontal ties option 3 requirements are very similar to CP 110:1972. In addition to this, full vertical ties need to be provided. This option further requires that the minimum thickness of wall should be 150 mm, which makes it a costly exercise. No doubt it would be difficult to provide reinforcements in 102.5 mm wall. However, there could be several ways whereby this problem could be overcome. This option is impracticable in brickwork although possibly feasible for hollow block walls.

Option 2: The only option left is No. 2, which can be used in this case. The horizontal ties as required by CP 110:1972 have to be provided in any case. In addition the designer has to prove that the vertical elements one at a time can be removed without causing collapse.

10.8.4 Design Calculations for Option 2: (BS 5628)
Horizontal Ties: Basic horizontal tie force, $F_t = 60$ kN or $20 + 4N_S$ whichever is less. N_S = number of storeys.

$$20 + 4N_S = 20 + 4 \times 7 = 48 \text{ kN} < 60 \text{ kN} \quad \text{Hence use 48 kN} \quad .$$

Design Tie Force: (Table 13 BS 5628)

a) *Peripheral ties:* Tie force, F_t = 48 kN

A_S required: $(48 \times 10^3)/250 = 192$ mm^2 .

Provide one 16 mm ϕ bar as peripheral tie (201 mm^2) at roof and each floor level uninterrupted, located in slab within 1.2 m of the edge of the building.

b) *Internal ties:* Design tie force F_t or $(F_t(G_K + Q_K))/7.5 \times L_a/5$ whichever is greater in the direction of span.

Tie force: $F_t = 48$ kN/m $> 48\ \dfrac{4.8\dagger + 1.5}{7.5} \times \dfrac{3}{5} = 24.2$ kN/m .

Therefore $F_t = 48$ kN/m

(Also note $L_a < 5 \times$ clear height $= 5 \times 2.85 = 14.25$ m).

Span of corridor slab is less than 3 m, hence is not considered.

Tie force normal to span, $F_t = 48$ kN/m.

Required $A_S\ =\ \dfrac{(48 \times 1000)}{250}\ =\ 192$ mm^2.

Provide 10 mm dia. bar at 400 mm centre to centre in both directions.

Area provided 196 mm^2 (satisfactory).

Internal ties should also be provided at each floor level in two directions approximately at right angles. These ties should be uninterrupted and anchored to the peripheral tie at both ends. It will be noted that reinforcement provided for other purposes, such as main and distribution steel, may be regarded as forming a part of, or whole of, peripheral and internal ties.

Ties to external walls: Considered only loadbearing walls designated as B.

Design tie force $= 2\,F_t$ or $(h/2.5)\,F_t$ whichever is less

                                         $= 2 \times 48$ kN/m or $(2.85/2.5) \times 48$

                                         $= 96$ kN/m or 54 kN/m,

therefore design tie force $= 54$ kN/m .

$\dagger$ (For the roof this is less).

Check Tie Connection to Masonry

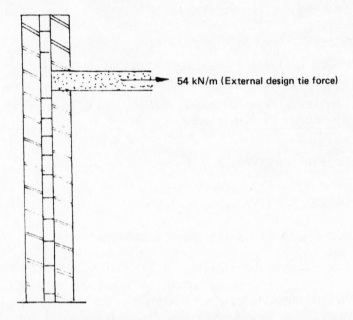

54 kN/m (External design tie force)

Ignoring the vertical load at the level under consideration, the design characteristic shear stress at the interface of masonry and concrete

$$= \frac{54 \times 10^3 \times \gamma_{mv}}{2 \times 102.5 \times 1000}$$

where γ_{mv} $= 1.25$ (clause 27.4 BS 5628)

$$= \frac{54 \times 10^3 \times 1.25}{2 \times 102.5 \times 1000}$$

$$= 0.33 \text{ N/mm}^2 < 0.35 \text{ N/mm}^2 \quad .$$

Hence it is satisfactory, and there is no need to provide external wall ties at any floor level. Further, the vertical load acting at any joint will increase the shear resistance as explained in section 9.5.2.4.

10.8.5 Vertical Elements

The designer needs to be satisfied that removal or wall A or B or C, one at a time, will not precipitate the collapse of the structure.

Definition of Terms used in Brickwork

Bed joint	Horizontal mortar joint
Bond	(1) pattern to which units are laid in a wall, usually to ensure that cross joints in adjoining courses are not in vertical alignment
	(2) adhesion of bricks and mortar
Cavity wall	two single-leaf walls spaced apart and tied together with wall ties
Chase	a groove formed or cut in a wall to accommodate pipes or cables
Collar joint	vertical joint in a bonded wall parallel to the face
Column	an isolated vertical compression member whose width is not less than four times its thickness
Course	a layer of brickwork including a mortar bed
Cross joint	a vertical joint at right angles to the face of a wall
Efflorescence	a deposit of salts on the surface of a wall left by evaporation
Fair-faced	a wall surface carefully finished with uniform jointing and even setting of bricks for good appearance
Frog	an indentation on the bedding surface of a brick
Grout	a mix consisting of cement, lime, sand and pea gravel with a sufficiently large water content to permit its being poured or pumped into cavities or pockets without the need for subsequent tamping or vibration
Header	a unit laid with its length at right angles to the face of the wall
Leaf	a wall, forming one skin of a cavity wall
Movement joint	a joint designed to permit relative longitudinal movement between contiguous sections of a wall in a building
Panel	an area of brickwork with defined boundaries, usually applied to walls resisting predominantly lateral loads
Perpend	the vertical joint in the face of a wall
Pier	a compression member formed by a thickened section of a wall

Pointing   the finishing of joints in the face of a wall carried out by raking out some of the mortar and re-filling either flush with the face or recessed in a particular way

Racking shear   a horizontal, in plane, force applied to a wall

Shear wall   a wall designed to resist horizontal, in plane forces e.g. wind loads

Spalling   a particular mode of failure of brickwork in which chips or large fragments generally parallel to the face of the brick are broken off

Stretcher   a unit laid with its length parallel to the face of the wall.

Notation

w	Uniformly distributed wind load/height
w_k	Characteristic wind load/area
W	Wind or lateral forces
G_k	Characteristic dead load
W_k	Characteristic wind load
Q_k	Characteristic live load
f_k	Characteristic compressive strength
A	Area of walls
E_x, E_y	Modulus of elasticity in x and y direction
E_m, E_b	Modulus of elasticity of brick and mortar
G	Modulus of rigidity
λ	Shear deformation coefficient or as described in the text
I	Second moment of area
Δ	Deflection or as described in the text
h	height of the building
x	distance of section under consideration from top or as specified in the text
e	Eccentricity of loading or distance of shear centre from centre line
L	Length of a wall
K	A constant or as described in the text
σ	Compressive stress
σ_b	Compressive stress in brick
σ_m	Compressive stress in mortar
ϵ	Elastic shortening
q_0, q_1, q_2	Transverse or lateral pressure
α	L/h or as specified in the text
k	A coefficient
M_x	Moment/unit width in x-direction (Parallel to bed joint)
M_y	Moment/unit width in y-direction (Perpendicular to bed joint)

Z	Sectional modulus
γ_{mv}	Material partial safety factor for shear
γ_m	Material partial safety factor
γ_f	Partial safety factor for the load
f_{ty}	Tensile strength normal to bed joint
f_{tx}	Tensile strength parallel to bed joint
f_{ky}, f_{kx}	Characteristic tensile strength normal and parallel to bed joints
β	A coefficient
μ	Orthotropy
m	Moment/unit length of fracture line
v_x, v_y	Poisson's ratios in x and y direction
v_b, v_m	Poisson's ratio for brick and mortar
μ_f	Coefficient of friction
V	Wind velocity
S_1, S_2, S_3	Factors (CP 3 Chapter V: Part 2)
F	Total wind force
C_p, C_{pi}	Coefficient of wind pressure
F_t	Tie force
A_S	Area of steel
N_S	Number of storeys

Further Reading and Reference

1. Sahlin, S., *Structural Masonry*, Prentice Hall, 1970.

2. Hendry, A. W., *Structural Brickwork*, Macmillan, 1981.

3. Handisyde, C. C. and Haseltine, B., *Bricks and Brickwork*, Brick Development Association, Windsor, Berks.

4. Gross, J. G., Dikkers, R. D. and Groggan, J. C., *Recommended Practice for Engineered Brick Masonry*, Brick Institute of America, McLean, Va., 1969.

5. Everett, A., *Mitchell's Building Construction*, Batsford, London.

6. Pearce, D. J. and Matthews, D. D., *Shear Walls (An appraisal of their design in box frame structures)*, Department of Environment, PSA, Croydon, U.K.

Index

A

accidental damage, 17, 62, 68, 138–146
accidental design, 175
accidents, probability of, 138
adhesion, brick-mortar, 51
alignment, deviation from, 53
axial force, tie beam, 121, 123, 125
axial loading, 69

B

beams, wall, 120
biaxial stress, 48, 49
bricks,
    absorption, 25
    Calculon, 21
    calcium silicate, 25, 28, 36
    compressive strength, 25
    classification, 20
    frost resistance, 25
    manufacturing control, 61
    salt content of, 21
    selection, 36
    soluble salt, 28
brickwork,
    advantages of, 13
    biaxial stress, 48
    characteristic strength, 59
    compressive strength, 39–46
    construction control, 61
    curing, 53
    efflorescence, 28
    fire resistance, 29
    moisture movement, 27
    shear strength, 47
    stress strain relation, 52
    sulphate attack, 29
    tensile strength, 50
    thermal expansion, 27
    workmanship effects, 53

C

calcium chloride, 33
capacity reduction factors, 62–65, 71
cavity wall, effective thickness, 74
cavity wall, design of, 81, 165
cellular wall arrangement, 14
characteristic strength, 18, 57, 59
characteristic loads, 18
codes of practice, 56
columns, design of, 29
column shear, 136
complex wall arrangements, 14
composite action, beams, 120–131
composite action, frame infil, 131–136
compression member design, 62–65
compressive strength, 39–46
concentrated loads, 65, 82
construction control, 61
cross-wall systems, 14

D

definition of terms, 179
design considerations, 13
design, strength, 18, 57
design vertical load resistance,
    of cavity construction, 81, 89
    of columns, 78
    of walls, 78, 86

E

eccentricity, 62, 70, 75, 85, 88
eccentric loading, 70
effective height, 71
effective thickness, 73
enhanced resistance, 72
expansion joints, 28
explosions, 138

F

failure theory, compression, 42–45
flexural tensile strength, 51
foundations, 19
fracture line analysis, 115
fracture line coefficients, 118
frame analysis, 77
frost inhibitors, 33
frost resistance, 25
frictional resistance, 146

J

joints, failure to fill, 53
joint material, effect of, 41
joint thickness, effect of, 44, 53

L

laterally loaded walls, 67
laterally loaded walls, design, 173
lime, 31
limit state principles, 18
load, characteristic, 18, 57
load, partial safety factor for, 58

M

masonry cement, 31
materials, partial safety factors for, 58
moments, plastic, 133, 134, 135
moments, wall-beams
        central, 121, 122, 129
        maximum, 121, 123, 129
mortar, 29–35
mortar consistency, 35
movement in brickwork, 27

N

notation, 180

P

partial safety factors, 18, 57, 58, 60
piers, 73, 74
pigment, 33
plasticiser, 33
Portland cement, 31
probability of failure, 18
progressive collapse, 68, 139–141
protected member, 68, 177

R

returns, effect of, 106–111
robustness, 17

S

sand, 33
settlement, 19
shear strength, 47
shear strength characteristic, 60
shear stress, wall-beams, 121, 123, 126
shear walls, 90–101
stability, 14, 15, 17, 61, 90
stress-strain properties, 52
structural safety, 17
suction, adjustment of, 54
sulphate attack, 29

T

tensile strength, direct, 50
tensile strength, flexural, 51, 60
ties, horizontal, 142
ties, internal, 143, 145
ties, peripheral, 143, 145
ties, vertical, 142
ties, wall, 35

V

vehicle impact, 138
vertical stress, wall-beam, 121, 124

W

wall beams, 121
wall design, calculations, 150
wall design,
        compression, 70, 78, 83–89
        lateral loading with precompression,
                104–113
        without precompression, 113–119
wall layout, 14
wall ties, 35
water, 33
wind load, design, 152
workmanship, 61
        effects of, 53

Y

yield line method, 115
Young's modulus, 52